EVALUATIONS FOR SENTENCING OF JUVENILES IN CRIMINAL COURT

BEST PRACTICES IN FORENSIC MENTAL HEALTH ASSESSMENT

Series Editors

Thomas Grisso, Alan M. Goldstein, and Kirk Heilbrun

Series Advisory Board

Paul Appelbaum, Richard Bonnie, and John Monahan

Titles in the Series

Foundations of Forensic Mental Health Assessment, *Kirk Heilbrun, Thomas Grisso, and Alan M. Goldstein*

Criminal Titles

Evaluation of Competence to Stand Trial, *Patricia A. Zapf and Ronald Roesch*
Evaluation of Criminal Responsibility, *Ira K. Packer*
Evaluation Capacity to Waive Miranda Rights, *Alan Goldstein and Naomi E. Sevin Goldstein*
Evaluation of Sexually Violent Predators, *Philip H. Witt and Mary Alice Conroy*
Evaluation for Risk of Violence in Adults, *Kirk Heilbrun*
Jury Selection, *Margaret Bull Kovera and Brian L. Cutler*
Evaluation for Capital Sentencing, *Mark D. Cunningham*
Evaluating Eyewitness Identification, *Brian L. Cutler and Margaret Bull Kovera*
Evaluations for Sentencing of Juveniles in Criminal Court, *Antoinette Kavanaugh and Thomas Grisso*

Civil Titles

Evaluation of Capacity to Consent to Treatment and Research, *Scott Y. H. Kim*
Evaluation for Guardianship, *Eric Y. Drogin and Curtis L. Barrett*
Evaluation for Personal Injury Claims, *Andrew W. Kane and Joel A. Dvoskin*
Evaluation for Civil Commitment, *Debra Pinals and Douglas Mossman*
Evaluation for Workplace Discrimination and Harassment, *Jane Goodman-Delahunty and William E. Foote*
Evaluation of Workplace Disability, *Lisa Drago Piechowski*
Evaluations of Police Suitability and Fitness for Duty, *David M. Corey and Mark Zelig*

Juvenile and Family Titles

Evaluation for Child Custody, *Geri S.W. Fuhrmann and Robert A. Zibbell*
Evaluation of Juveniles' Competence to Stand Trial, *Ivan Kruh and Thomas Grisso*
Evaluation for Risk of Violence in Juveniles, *Robert Hoge and D.A. Andrews*
Evaluation of Parenting Capacity in Child Protection, *Karen S. Budd, Jennifer Clark, and Mary A. Connell*

EVALUATIONS FOR SENTENCING OF JUVENILES IN CRIMINAL COURT

ANTOINETTE KAVANAUGH

THOMAS GRISSO

OXFORD
UNIVERSITY PRESS

OXFORD
UNIVERSITY PRESS

Oxford University Press is a department of the University of Oxford. It furthers the University's objective of excellence in research, scholarship, and education by publishing worldwide. Oxford is a registered trade mark of Oxford University Press in the UK and certain other countries.

Published in the United States of America by Oxford University Press
198 Madison Avenue, New York, NY 10016, United States of America.

Library of Congress Cataloging-in-Publication Data
Names: Kavanaugh, Antoinette, author | Grisso, Thomas, author.
Title: Evaluations for sentencing of juveniles in criminal court /
Antoinette Kavanaugh, Thomas Grisso.
Other titles: Best practices in forensic mental health assessment.
Description: New York, NY : Oxford University Press, [2021] |
Series: Best practices in forensic mental health assessment |
Includes bibliographical references and index.
Identifiers: LCCN 2020011516 (print) | LCCN 2020011517 (ebook) |
ISBN 9780190052812 (paperback) | ISBN 9780190052836 (epub) |
ISBN 9780190052843
Subjects: LCSH: Juvenile justice, Administration of—United States. |
Juvenile delinquents—Legal status, laws, etc.—United States. |
Juvenile delinquents—Mental health services—United States. |
Pre-sentence investigation reports—United States. |
Forensic psychology—United States.
Classification: LCC KF9779.K38 2021 (print) |
LCC KF9779 (ebook) | DDC 345.73/087—dc23
LC record available at https://lccn.loc.gov/2020011516
LC ebook record available at https://lccn.loc.gov/2020011517

9 8 7 6 5 4 3 2 1

Printed by Marquis, Canada

Contents

About Best Practices in Forensic Mental Health Assessment

The recent growth of the fields of forensic psychology and forensic psychiatry has created a need for this book series describing best practices in forensic mental health assessment (FMHA). Currently, forensic evaluations are conducted by mental health professionals for a variety of criminal, civil, and juvenile legal questions. The research foundation supporting these assessments has become broader and deeper in recent decades. Consensus has become clearer on the recognition of requirements for ethical and professional conduct. In the larger context of the current emphasis on "empirically supported" assessment and intervention in psychiatry and psychology, the specialization of FMHA has advanced sufficiently to justify a series devoted to best practices. Although this series focuses mainly on evaluations conducted by psychologists and psychiatrists, the fundamentals and principles offered also apply to evaluations conducted by clinical social workers, psychiatric nurses, and other mental health professionals.

This series describes "best practice" as empirically supported (when the relevant research is available), legally relevant, and consistent with applicable ethical and professional standards. Authors of the books in this series identify the approaches that seem best, while incorporating what is practical and acknowledging that best practice represents a goal to which the forensic clinician should aspire, rather than a standard that can always be met. The American Academy of Forensic Psychology assisted the editors in enlisting the consultation of board-certified forensic psychologists specialized in each topic area. Board-certified forensic psychiatrists were also consultants on many of the volumes. Their comments on the manuscripts helped to ensure that the methods described in these volumes represent a generally accepted view of best practice.

The series' authors were selected for their specific expertise in a particular area. At the broadest level, however, certain general principles apply to all types of forensic evaluations. Rather than repeat those fundamental principles in every volume, the series offers them in the first volume, *Foundations of Forensic Mental Health Assessment*. Reading the first book, followed by a specific topical book, will provide the reader both the general principles that the specific topic shares with all forensic evaluations and those that are particular to the specific assessment question.

The specific topics of the 21 books were selected by the series editors as the most important and oft-considered areas of forensic assessment conducted by mental health professionals and behavioral scientists. Each of the 21 topical books is organized according to a common template. The authors address the applicable legal context, forensic mental health concepts, and empirical foundations and limits in the "Foundation" part of the book. They then describe preparation for the evaluation, data collection, data interpretation, and report writing and testimony in the "Application" part of the book. This creates a fairly uniform approach to considering these areas across different topics. All authors in this series have attempted to be as concise as possible in addressing best practice in their area. In addition, topical volumes feature elements to make them user friendly in actual practice. These elements include boxes that highlight especially important information, relevant case law, best-practice guidelines, and cautions against common pitfalls.

We hope the series will be useful for different groups of individuals. Practicing forensic clinicians will find succinct, current information relevant to their practice. Those who are in training to specialize in FMHA (whether in formal training or in the process of respecialization) should find helpful the combination of broadly applicable considerations presented in the first volume together with the more specific aspects of other volumes in the series. Those who teach and supervisee trainees can offer these volumes as a guide for practices to which the trainee can aspire. Researchers and scholars interested in FMHA best practice may find researchable ideas, particularly on topics that have received insufficient research attention to date. Judges and attorneys with questions about FMHA best practice will find these books relevant and concise. Clinical and forensic administrators who run agencies, court clinics, and hospitals in which litigants are assessed may also use some of the books in this series to establish expectancies for evaluations performed by professionals in their agencies.

We also anticipate that the 21 specific books in this series will serve as reference works that help courts and attorneys evaluate the quality of forensic mental health professionals' evaluations. A word of caution is in order, however. These volumes focus on best practice, not what is minimally acceptable legally or ethically. Courts involved in malpractice litigation, or ethics committees or licensure boards considering complaints, should not expect that materials describing best practice easily or necessarily translate into the minimally acceptable professional conduct that is typically at issue in such proceedings.

The idea for the present book was developed following decisions by the U.S. Supreme Court in *Miller v. Alabama* and *Montgomery v. Louisiana*. In those decisions, the Court made it clear that individuals convicted of offenses occurring prior to age 18 could not receive a sentence of mandatory life without parole. This raised important questions. Would these decisions apply retroactively to those convicted before they were decided? (The short answer is yes. See *Montgomery*.) How would sentencing courts determine the sentence for future individuals convicted? How would courts decide on a new sentence for those originally given mandatory life without parole? These complex questions can be informed by developmentally sensitive FMHA. In the second of two books published in this series following a several-year hiatus, Kavanaugh and Grisso use a developmental lens to describe a new approach to FMHA that is critically important in light of *Miller* and *Montgomery*. This is the first book to offer guidance to forensic mental health examiners when performing evaluations to assist attorneys and judges in *Miller* sentencing and resentencing cases. We expect that it will be extraordinarily helpful to those involved in evaluations and decisions regarding the sentencing or resentencing of individuals convicted of serious crimes committed before the age of 18.

Kirk Heilbrun
Alan Goldstein
Thomas Grisso

Acknowledgment

We would like to thank the editors of this book series: Kirk Heilbrun, PhD, and Alan Goldstein, PhD, as well as those who generously gave their time to review this book. We also want to thank Bryan Stevenson for his courage and fortitude to challenge the US Supreme Court to recognize the developmental differences between youth and adults.

From Dr. Grisso:
I wish to acknowledge and thank my colleagues in the MacArthur Research Network on Adolescent Development and Juvenile Justice for their collaborative work across the years. That work provided much of the science related to adolescents' capacities, competencies, and culpability in legal contexts.

From Dr. Kavanaugh:
I am forever grateful for the support, time, and mental space Lisa and Cooper gave me to accomplish this task. This work is in memory of my grandmother Mildred and my great-aunt Doris, two women who encouraged me to make a space for myself in this world. Finally, I want to recognize that at the time of publication, we are living in a world that vibrates to the words of Dr. Martin Luther King: "A riot is the language of the unheard."

1 The Legal Context

This book is a guide for forensic evaluations in cases in which clinicians are asked to provide information for the sentencing of a juvenile found guilty in criminal court for a crime. The purpose of these assessments is to assist the court in weighing developmental and clinical factors related to mitigation in sentencing for juvenile crimes under criminal law. All states provide for juvenile offenders to be tried in criminal court as adults for certain offenses allegedly committed while they were of juvenile age—in most states, less than age 18. States' laws often allow this for certain serious offenses, either by discretionary transfer by a juvenile court judge or as a statutory mandate (Heilbrun et al., 2017).

A juvenile transferred to criminal court and found guilty is subject to sentencing according to the state's allowable sentences for the crime committed, just as adult defendants are. For some crimes, criminal court sentences for adults are mandatory (e.g., the death penalty or life without parole [LWOP] for certain kinds of homicide convictions). In other circumstances, judges must determine a sentence at their discretion, often within a minimum and maximum time set by law.

When sentences are discretionary, defense attorneys may provide evidence to establish mitigating circumstances for the judge to consider at the time of sentencing. As discussed later in this chapter, for juvenile offenders, courts are constitutionally required to consider potentially mitigating evidence regarding a youth's mental and developmental characteristics that could reduce culpability. When immaturity/maturity is at issue in this context, forensic clinical examiners may be asked to evaluate the defendant to offer expert opinion on these characteristics of the defendant.

Legal and Forensic Scope of the Book

Until recent years, there was no constitutional requirement that courts consider immaturity as mitigation of culpability in sentencing for juvenile crimes in criminal court. This changed dramatically with a series of U.S. Supreme Court decisions between 2005 and 2016. In these cases, the Court ruled that judges *must* give special consideration to juveniles when sentenced in criminal court in homicide cases. The court prohibited the death penalty for homicide (*Roper v. Simmons*, 2005), prohibited LWOP for non-homicide offenses (*Graham v. Florida*, 2010), prohibited *mandatory* LWOP in juvenile homicide cases (*Miller v. Alabama*, 2012), and applied *Miller* retroactively, requiring resentencing for many persons currently serving LWOP sentences (*Montgomery v. Louisiana*, 2016). The Court ruled that sentencing in homicide cases must consider certain characteristics of youth for potential mitigation when deciding on LWOP and alternative sentences.

This book applies the requirements that the U.S. Supreme Court established in *Miller* and *Montgomery* for considering immaturity as mitigation in criminal court LWOP sentencing for juvenile homicide cases. However, the developmental framework that the Court established, and the general concepts and methods described in this book, are not necessarily limited to *Miller* or *Montgomery* homicide cases. Legal scholars (e.g., Scott et al., 2016) have argued that *Miller* created a constitutional requirement that applies to all juvenile sentencing in criminal court, not only *Miller* cases.

As a consequence, the evaluation concepts and methods described here can be used with youth being sentenced in criminal court for a charge other than homicide. Moreover, some states do not allow LWOP under any circumstances for juveniles charged in criminal court, yet they may still receive very long sentences, some exceeding life expectancy (see "Alternative Sentences" later in this chapter). Therefore, although structured for *Miller* and *Montgomery* evaluations, the concepts, research, and methods in this book offer a guide for evaluating *any* juvenile charged in criminal court, when information related to developmental mitigation in sentencing is requested.

Evaluations Under *Miller* and *Montgomery*

The U.S. Supreme Court decisions noted earlier have given rise to what are commonly referred to as "*Miller* evaluations." Broadly construed, a *Miller* evaluation is any forensic evaluation designed to provide legal decision makers with relevant information about the individual sentenced (or to be sentenced) in criminal court for an offense committed as a juvenile, with or without LWOP as an optional sentence. *Miller* evaluations occur in two basic contexts: (a) *Miller sentencing* immediately after adjudication (although sentencing evaluations may occur prior to the adjudication) and (b) *Miller resentencing* as required by *Montgomery*, involving those who have been serving LWOP sentences for past homicides as juveniles. The *Miller* decision and its criteria apply to both types of cases, so this book refers to them collectively as "*Miller* cases," but with the modifiers "sentencing" or "resentencing" to distinguish them. Much of what courts must consider is similar for both *Miller* sentencing and resentencing cases, but methods and procedures of evaluations for the two will be different in various respects, as will be described throughout this book.

Socio-Legal History

It is helpful to know the socio-legal context of the Court's recent decisions on sentencing of juveniles in criminal court. Of relevance are the historical relation of the juvenile court to criminal court, as well as events leading to the U.S. Supreme Court's decisions.

Relation of Juvenile Court to Criminal Court

The juvenile court in the United States began 120 years ago with recognition that youth (then identified as younger than 16 or 17 years of age) were different from adults in their motivations, capacities, and potential for rehabilitation when they committed illegal acts (Tanenhaus, 2004). Instead of subjecting young offenders to adult penalties, the juvenile court promised to provide rehabilitative opportunities. For very serious felonies, however, exceptions were made when it appeared that the youth had developed criminal attitudes and behavior not likely to change given the juvenile justice system's resources. In such cases, juvenile courts could waive their jurisdiction and transfer the youth to criminal court for trial and potential sentencing as an adult.

In the 1960s, the U.S. Supreme Court (*Kent v. U.S.*, 1966) required that the procedures used in juvenile courts for deciding on transfer to criminal court must satisfy basic requirements of due process and fairness associated with the serious consequences of transfer for juveniles. A year later, in *In re Gault* (1967), the Court affirmed that youth who were arrested and interrogated by law enforcement officers were protected by the right to avoid self-incrimination. Together these two cases ushered in a new era of due process rights for youth in juvenile court. Youth were now to be provided access to legal counsel and hearings that more formally adhered to rules of procedural fairness. As applied to transfer hearings, the state was required to provide evidence related to specific criteria showing that the youth could not be rehabilitated within the juvenile justice system (e.g., dangerousness, sophistication-maturity, and prospects for rehabilitation) (Grisso, 2013; Heilbrun et al., 2017).

During the 1980s and 1990s, the United States experienced a significant increase in serious youthful offending, which contributed to a dramatic increase in the punitiveness of juvenile laws in almost all states in response to youth crime (Grisso, 1996). Most states changed their laws to make transfer to criminal court easier and more frequent. During that time, the number of youths transferred to criminal court increased 64% nationally (Butts & Travis, 2002), exposing many thousands of youth to adult sentences, including the possibility of the death penalty or LWOP.

Recent Juvenile Justice Reform

Early in the 21st century, several factors contributed to a change in public perceptions and attitudes regarding the recent punitive reform and widespread transfer of youth to criminal court for sentencing. The reasons included (a) a steadily falling rate of violent crimes by youth, (b) concerns about racial disproportionality in the use of transfer, and (c) rising costs of the punitive reform's high incarceration rates. In addition, the period 1995 to 2010 witnessed a wave of new neuroscientific and behavioral evidence demonstrating specifically how youths' brain-and-behavior development was immature in relation to adults in ways that suggested their lesser culpability for offenses (for reviews, see Steinberg, 2013; Scott & Steinberg, 2008).

The impact of this research on 21st-century U.S. juvenile justice policy was substantial, as seen in federal policy recommendations (e.g., National Academies of Science, 2013) and in four U.S. Supreme Court decisions from 2005 to 2016. As discussed in the next section, these cases all recognized youths' developmental immaturity relative to that of adults; they required that developmental characteristics of adolescence be considered as potentially mitigating factors when determining criminal court sentences for serious crimes committed by juveniles.

U.S. Supreme Court Cases on Sentencing of Juveniles in Criminal Court

The four U.S. Supreme Court cases relevant for understanding the Court's logic related to *Miller* sentencing and resentencing cases are *Roper v. Simmons* (2005), *Graham v. Florida* (2010), *Miller v. Alabama* (2012), and *Montgomery v. Louisiana* (2016). A fifth case during this era, *J.D.B. v. North Carolina* (2011), did not involve sentencing but followed much of the same developmental logic as the other four cases. The following brief review of the cases and their use of developmental science is discussed in greater detail elsewhere (see, e.g., Levick & Feierman, 2016).

From *Roper* to *Montgomery*

The Court's four juvenile sentencing cases limited criminal court sentencing for serious crimes by juveniles in the following ways: (a) *Roper* prohibited the death penalty; (b) *Graham* prohibited

LWOP in non-homicide cases; (c) *Miller* prohibited mandatory LWOP sentences in homicide cases; and (d) *Montgomery* required resentencing for cases of persons currently serving mandatory LWOP sentences for homicides as juveniles. All four cases were decided based on the Court's interpretation of the Eighth Amendment's prohibition of cruel and unusual punishment. All four cases based their interpretation of "cruel and unusual" in part on the Court's consideration of adolescents' developmental immaturity, relative to adults, in terms of their lesser capacities for decision making and judgment, as well as their vulnerability associated with their dependency. These considerations, the Court said, offered potential mitigation for juveniles' culpability as a class.

The four cases differed, however, in some important respects. *Roper, Miller*, and *Montgomery* applied to homicide cases, *Graham* to non-homicide cases. *Roper* (death) and *Graham* (LWOP) prohibited specific sentences, while *Miller* and *Montgomery* did not prohibit LWOP for homicide. They allowed it so long as sentencing proceedings (for LWOP or alternative sentences) offered adequate consideration of potentially mitigating factors related to adolescents' immaturity.

The Logic of *Miller* and *Montgomery*

In its decision in *Miller*, the Court articulated its reasons for considering adolescents' immaturity as a potentially mitigating factor in homicide cases. Its reasoning followed and cited *Roper* and *Graham*, and the following language from *Miller* captures the Court's logic:

> As to the first set of cases: *Roper* and *Graham* establish that children are constitutionally different from adults for sentencing purposes. Their lack of maturity and underdeveloped sense of responsibility lead to recklessness, impulsivity, and heedless risk-taking. They are more vulnerable to negative influences and outside pressures, including from their family and peers; they have limited control over their own environment and lack the ability to extricate themselves from horrific, crime-producing settings.

> And because a child's character is not as well formed as an adult's, his traits are less fixed and his actions are less likely to be evidence of irretrievable depravity. *Roper* and *Graham* emphasized that the distinctive attributes of youth diminish the penological justifications for imposing the harshest sentences on juvenile offenders, even when they commit terrible crimes. (*Miller v. Alabama*, 2012, p. 2458)

Given these general characteristics of adolescence, the Court in *Miller* noted that LWOP could be assigned only to the "rare juvenile offender whose crime reflects irreparable corruption" (*Miller v. Alabama*, 2012, p. 2469). The Court underscored this in *Montgomery*, reserving LWOP in juvenile homicide cases for only "the rarest of juvenile offenders, those whose crimes reflect permanent incorrigibility," which would exclude "the vast majority of juveniles" (*Montgomery v. Louisiana*, 2016, p. 734). Moreover, the Court required that in juvenile homicide cases where LWOP might be considered, any alternative sentences must consider the developmental characteristics of a youth.

Implications of *Miller* and *Montgomery*

To date there are no data on the frequency of *Miller* sentencing cases or forensic evaluations to assist them. In addition, the Court made no specific mention of the need for expert developmental, clinical, or forensic evaluations in such cases. Yet the nature of the developmental characteristics in question clearly points to the high likelihood that parties in most *Miller* sentencing cases will seek expert evaluations to assist the court in weighing mitigating developmental factors of adolescence in an individualized, case-by-case manner. It is also likely that attorneys will request evaluations in non-homicide cases that allow judicial discretion in length of sentences. In addition, evaluations may be requested for use in parole board hearings as well in some *Montgomery* cases.

The *Montgomery* decision, requiring some of the same types of information, creates a particular challenge in that resentencing may include consideration of the person's developmental characteristics at the time of the original sentencing. The subject of the evaluation usually will be an adult who has been serving an LWOP sentence for some years. *Miller* resentencing cases will also require different types of data than *Miller* sentencing cases, especially related to rehabilitation progress during the person's incarceration.

According to a nationwide survey, between 2,000 and 2,500 individuals were serving mandatory LWOP terms for juvenile homicide around the time of the *Miller* and *Montgomery* decisions (Mills et al., 2016). In addition, several states have decided that *Miller* resentencing cases must be provided for those who received not only mandatory LWOP but also discretionary LWOP sentences. Thus, the demand for forensic evaluations in *Miller* resentencing cases might continue for some years.

Since *Miller*, many states' legislatures or state supreme courts have decided to abolish LWOP for juvenile offenses altogether. By 2018, 25 states and the District of Columbia had done so (Campaign for Fair Sentencing of Youth, 2018; for an example, see the State of Washington Supreme Court decision in *State v. Bassett*, 2018). Other states are expected to follow this trend in the future. In those states, formal *Miller* hearings will disregard LWOP as a sentencing alternative. Nevertheless, *Miller*-type evaluations will continue to be relevant because the alternative sentences for juvenile homicide are lengthy and will still require judicial consideration of potentially mitigating developmental factors (Scott et al., 2016).

Factors to Be Considered for Juvenile Sentencing in Criminal Court

Miller provided a set of five developmental factors that must be reviewed when considering LWOP or alternative sentences in juvenile homicide cases. In addition, *Miller* and *Montgomery* said that a condition of "irreparable corruption" was required to justify providing an LWOP sentence for juvenile homicide. Here we review these factors and concepts that form the basis for *Miller* sentencing and resentencing cases.

Mitigating Characteristics of Adolescence ("*Miller* Factors")

Using the logic of *Roper* and *Graham, Miller* and *Montgomery* identified several characteristics of adolescence to describe how youth are immature relative to adults, supporting the Court's conclusion that children are different from, and less culpable than, adults for sentencing purposes. These same characteristics of adolescent immaturity, the Court said, must be applied to each individual case, examining them for their potential mitigation of culpability. Therefore, characteristics of immaturity described by the Court offer a potential structure for *Miller* evaluations, including nonhomicide cases and cases in which sentences other than LWOP are being considered. Four types of evidence are relevant, as described in this section, and a fifth factor is ambiguous as to whether it must be weighed individually in *Miller* sentencing cases.

Miller and *Montgomery* described each of these characteristics only briefly and did not provide the labels for the *Miller* factors offered in the present analysis. The labels used in this section parallel those offered in other commentaries that have translated legally relevant adolescent immaturity as described in the *Miller* decision (Grisso & Kavanaugh, 2016; Scott et al., 2015). These concepts are elaborated in Chapter 2, employing scientific evidence that the Court itself used to identify the factors.

Examiners should be aware that some state courts have begun to fashion their own lists and categories of developmental factors much like *Miller*'s (e.g., *People v. Gutierrez*, 2014). Typically, they will be variations on *Miller*'s factors that are quite similar. Absent local variations, the factors described in *Miller* and reviewed here are likely to apply.

DECISIONAL IMMATURITY (DECISIONAL FACTOR)

Youth are immature compared to adults in capacities associated with decision making, delay of impulse, and consideration of consequences of one's decision. The Court described their decisional immaturity as an "underdeveloped sense of responsibility, leading to recklessness, impulsivity, and heedless risk-taking" (*Miller v. Alabama*, 2012, p. 2458, citing *Roper*). Other phrases used in *Miller* regarding decisional immaturity include "transient rashness, proclivity for risk, and inability to assess consequences" (p. 2465) and "immaturity, impetuosity, and failure to appreciate risks and consequences" (p. 2468).

DEPENDENCE ON FAMILY AND ENVIRONMENT (DEPENDENCY FACTOR)

Youth are more vulnerable and less autonomous than adults, limiting their capacity to avoid harmful circumstances. Describing this factor, *Miller* noted, "Children are more vulnerable to negative influences and outside pressures, including from their family and peers; they have limited control over their own environment and lack the ability to extricate themselves from horrific, crime-producing settings" (*Miller v. Alabama*, 2012, p. 2458, in part citing *Roper*). In addition, *Miller* indicated that courts must "take into account the family and home environment that surrounds him—and from which he cannot extricate himself—no matter how brutal or dysfunctional" (*Miller v. Alabama*, 2012, p. 2458). The Court's description of the appellant Evan Miller clarifies the Court's meaning regarding this factor: "Miller's stepfather physically abused him; his alcoholic and drug-addicted mother neglected him; he had been in and out of foster care as a result; and he had tried to kill himself four times, the first when he should have been in kindergarten" (*Miller v. Alabama*, 2012, p. 2469).

CONSIDERATION OF OFFENSE CONTEXT (OFFENSE CONTEXT FACTOR)

The Court called for consideration of "the circumstances of the homicide offense, including the extent of [the youth's] participation in the conduct and the way familial and peer pressures may have affected him" (*Miller v. Alabama*, 2012, p. 2468). The Court seemed to anticipate using information about the youth's status on the decisional and dependency factors to analyze the offense circumstances, examining the nature of the youth's involvement as this might affect mitigation. How planned or impulsive was the youth's participation? To what extent was the youth's decision making prior to and during the offense related to past abuses or present peer influences? For example, in *Miller* the Court reflected on Miller's co-appellant Jackson, noting that he "learned on the way to the video store that his friend Shields was carrying a gun, but his age could well have affected his calculation of the risk that posed, as well as his willingness to walk away at that point" (*Miller v. Alabama*, 2012, p. 2468).

DEFENDANT'S PROSPECTS FOR REHABILITATION (PROSPECTS FOR REHABILITATION FACTOR)

The Court required that sentencing take into consideration a youth's characteristics related to the potential or capacity for change through rehabilitation, treatment, and/or maturation. "A child's character is not as well formed as an adult's; his traits are less fixed" (*Miller v. Alabama*, 2012, p. 2458). Thus, *Montgomery* explained, "*Miller* required that sentencing courts consider a child's . . . heightened capacity for change" (*Montgomery v. Louisiana*, 2016, p. 726) on an individualized, case-by-case basis.

RISK OF INCOMPETENCY DURING LEGAL PROCESS (LEGAL COMPETENCY FACTOR)

Addressing why juveniles as a class should not receive mandatory LWOP sentences, *Miller* explained that juveniles "might have been charged and convicted of a lesser offense if not for incompetencies associated with youth—for example, his inability to deal with police officers or prosecutors (including a plea agreement) or his incapacity to assist his own attorneys" (*Miller v. Alabama*, 2012, p. 2468, citing *Graham*). The Court's concern was with immature characteristics of adolescence that create a disadvantage during the investigative and adjudicative processes, potentially placing adolescents in the position of eligibility for a lengthy sentence they might not otherwise have faced.

However, *Miller* and *Montgomery* do not address whether this matter should be weighed individually (that is, on a case-by-case basis) when considering sentences. It appears to have been included primarily to support the argument against *mandatory* sentencing for juveniles as a class. For this reason, it is not offered here as a factor routinely applied to evaluations of sentencing in individual cases.

Irreparable Corruption

Miller and *Montgomery* prohibited LWOP for juvenile crimes except for those "rarest" of youth who are irreparably corrupt. The Court used other labels for the concept that are assumed to be synonymous: "irretrievably depraved" (*Miller v. Alabama*, 2012, p. 2469) and "permanent incorrigibility" (*Montgomery v. Louisiana*, 2016, p. 734). *Montgomery* added that an LWOP sentence could be given only to juvenile homicide offenders who "exhibit such irretrievable depravity that rehabilitation is impossible" (*Montgomery v. Louisiana*, 2016, p. 734).

Miller did not require a specific finding of facts regarding a youth's irreparable corruption. *Montgomery* explained that this did not relieve courts from applying irreparable corruption as a necessary condition for LWOP (see *Montgomery v. Louisiana*, 2016, pp. 19–20). Consequently, *Miller* and *Montgomery* left to the discretion of the states the task of deciding how they would apply the requirement. Thus, the Court did not provide a specific definition or criteria for deciding irreparable corruption. (But see *Jones v. Mississippi*, 2019, under review by the U.S. Supreme Court as this book was in press.)

As noted, about half of the states subsequently decided to abolish LWOP for juvenile crimes. In those states, no application of irreparable corruption is required. The remainder of the states have discretion regarding how they interpret the requirement. One must consult a state's statutes, case law, and/or practice to identify how the concept is applied in *Miller* sentencing and resentencing cases in that jurisdiction.

Montgomery and a few subsequent state appellate cases suggest some boundaries or limits when interpreting the meaning of irreparable corruption. First, *Montgomery* (citing *Roper*) affirmed that "children who commit even heinous crimes are capable of change" (*Montgomery v. Louisiana*, 2016, 736). This suggests that irreparable corruption cannot be concluded based on the nature of the crime itself. Second, some state courts addressing irreparable corruption have concluded that the condition is not determined simply by the defendant's degree of maturity. For example, the Georgia Supreme Court concluded that irreparable corruption depends not on "a consideration of his age and the qualities that accompany youth . . . but rather on a specific determination that he is irreparably corrupt" (*Veal v. State*, 2016, p. 411). In other words, evidence that one is developmentally mature (e.g., adult-like and a frequent offender) and has committed a heinous murder is not synonymous with irreparable corruption.

Solely by inference, the words used by the U.S. Supreme Court to label and describe the "rarest of youth" as irreparably corrupt suggest that this is (a) a condition (corruption, depravity, or incorrigibility) that (b) promotes lifetime offending and (c) cannot be changed (irreparable, permanent, or irretrievable) (d) by any means (e.g., punishment, therapeutic intervention, education, or maturation).

Alternative Sentences

The limits that the U.S. Supreme Court placed on LWOP for juvenile sentencing have caused the states to begin fashioning alternative sentences, and they vary considerably across states. As reviewed by Scott et al. (2015), laws establishing minimum sentences for juvenile homicide tend to range from 15 to 20 years. Maximum limits sometimes add another 15 to 20 years, but, at times, they are so high that they could exceed the statistical life expectancy of most juveniles convicted of homicide. Sentencing options often allow for judicial discretion in length of time to eligibility for parole. For example, for first-degree murder in juvenile cases, Massachusetts instructs that "the court shall fix a minimum term of not less than 20 years nor more than 30 years," although the minimum must be 25 years if the court finds that the murder was committed "with deliberately premeditated malice aforethought" (Mass. Gen. Laws Ann., ch. 279, § 24).

Special issues arise in cases in which youth have been convicted of homicide together with other offenses, each of which has a specified length of sentence. Courts often have the option to allow those sentences to be served concurrently, typically based on the offense with the longest sentence. Alternatively, often state law allows the court to rule that multiple sentences are to be served consecutively.

When served consecutively, sentences for homicide with additional offenses have sometimes exceeded the life expectancy of the individual, creating what are called *de facto* life sentences.

Some courts have decided that *de facto* life sentences for juvenile homicide cases violate the intent of the U.S. Supreme Court in *Graham v. Florida*'s (2010) requirement to provide "a meaningful opportunity to obtain release" (p. 50). For example, in *McKinley v. Butler* (2016), a federal appeals court decided that a 100-year consecutive term of sentences for a juvenile with homicide plus firearms convictions was the unconstitutional equivalent of an LWOP sentence. Similarly, the Supreme Court of Oregon (*White v. Premo*, 2019) found a sentence that would allow the defendant no option for parole until age 81 was life-equivalent, violating the intent of *Miller*. Some courts that have considered this question, however, have ruled that only an actual life sentence is barred by *Miller* (see Hoesterey, 2017, for a review of these cases).

Legal Process in *Miller* Sentencing Hearings

Several aspects of jurisdiction and procedure offer relevant background and context for examiners in *Miller* sentencing assessments (*Miller* resentencing is considered in a subsequent section). Of relevance are (a) age of eligibility, (b) court processing prior to sentencing, and (c) rules for sentencing hearings (e.g., burden and standard of proof).

Age

Miller sentencing cases involve juveniles who have been transferred (waived) to criminal court for trial and found guilty. Many states have an age below which one cannot be transferred, most often 10, 12, or 14, although some states have no statutory minimum age for transfer. Most states define the upper age of juvenile jurisdiction as the 17th or 18th birthday. Age of offense in *Miller* sentencing (and resentencing) cases, therefore, most often will be 14 through 17.

A few appellate cases have begun to apply *Miller*'s logic (mitigation related to developmental immaturity) to young adults (not transferred juveniles) whose homicides were committed when they were between 18 and 21 (e.g., *People v. Harris*, 2017; *People v. House*, 2015; *Sharp v. State*, 2014; *State v. O'Dell*, 2015). Pending other legal developments in such cases, we presume that courts hearing them will require the same types of developmental and mental health information as in *Miller* cases involving juveniles.

Trial Process

Guilt typically will be determined at a jury trial (unless the defendant has waived that right). *Miller* did not require consideration of developmental factors at adjudication, so *Miller* evaluations are unlikely to be requested for the trial stage of the proceedings. However, *Miller* examiners should be aware of certain steps in the adjudicative trial process that may be relevant for their evaluations for the sentencing phase.

The youth typically will have arrived in criminal court by transfer (waiver) based on a juvenile court judge's discretion, a prosecutor's discretion, or a state statute that automatically excludes certain serious offenses from juvenile court jurisdiction. Especially in cases of judicial transfer, youth may have been in juvenile court detention for many months. They also may have been evaluated by a forensic mental health expert during that transfer process. If they reached criminal court by statutory exclusion ("automatic transfer"), a reverse-waiver hearing may have occurred in criminal court in those states that allow waiver downward to juvenile court (Heilbrun et al., 2017). That hearing might have considered developmental immaturity in a manner similar to *Miller*'s. The individual may have been in custody during the juvenile court and/or criminal court process, from arraignment to adjudication, for up to two years. Thus, at the time one performs a *Miller* sentencing evaluation, the individual often will be a young adult (older than 17) because of time elapsed during the trial process.

Sentencing Process

The sentencing hearing occurs after adjudication, often with a delay between those hearings. A judge will hear evidence and decide the sentence. Juries are not used in sentencing except in a handful of states. Prosecution and defense may have agreed on a sentencing recommendation to the court, or they may have agreed in part while leaving disagreements to oral argument. For example, a prosecutor may decide not to seek LWOP but may want to contest defense arguments about developmental mitigation regarding the length of an alternative sentence. Oral arguments will proceed according to the rules of the court of jurisdiction.

How courts structure hearings on the evidence for the two questions may vary across states differing on the matter of burdens of proof regarding irreparable corruption. Appellate decisions on this matter have been mixed. Most courts addressing the issue have concluded that *Miller*'s and *Montgomery*'s observation that youth are "rarely" irreparably corrupt creates a rebuttable presumption that the youth is *not* irreparably corrupt (see, e.g., *U.S. v. Briones*, 2019, a Ninth Circuit case). This would place the burden on the prosecution to show that a youth is the exception (e.g., *Commonwealth v. Batts*, 2017: Pennsylvania). Other courts, however, have concluded that the U.S. Supreme Court did not go that far, thus placing the burden on the defense (e.g., *State v. Ramos*, 2017: Washington). (For further discussion, see Hoesterey, 2017.)

Some courts have concluded that the two questions (developmental mitigation regarding alternative sentences and irreparable corruption) should be kept separate because they rely on different types of evidence. For example, Georgia's Supreme Court (*Veal v. State*, 2016) observed that the irreparable corruption decision depends not on the court's consideration of developmental maturity or immaturity, but on whether the youth is *irreparably corrupt*—that is, a lifetime offender who cannot be rehabilitated. Other courts have agreed, noting that *Miller* presumes that most youth can be rehabilitated, and that arguments that the youth is "mature" cannot be used as an aggravating circumstance to support irreparable corruption (e.g., *State v. Null*, 2013; *State v. Seats*, 2015, citing *Miller*, 2012, p. 467–469; see Grisso & Kavanaugh, 2016, for further discussion). It is likely, however, that most courts will allow all evidence to be presented at once, rather than bifurcating the hearing to consider evidence for irreparable corruption separately from evidence for alternative sentences.

Legal Process in *Miller* Resentencing Hearings

Montgomery required a judicial reconsideration of the sentences of all individuals currently serving mandatory LWOP for crimes committed as juveniles. Even before *Montgomery*, some states had assumed that *Miller* should apply retroactively. As states began to address these cases, two major issues arose: (a) whether *Miller* resentencing was required only for prisoners who had received *mandatory* LWOP sentences and (b) the specific procedural approach for achieving *Montgomery*'s intent.

LWOP Sentences Eligible for Resentencing Review

While *Montgomery* required resentencing for all prisoners serving mandatory LWOP sentences for juvenile homicide, might resentencing also be required for prisoners serving *discretionary* LWOP sentences? Some courts have decided that it is (e.g., *Commonwealth v. Batts*, 2017, Pennsylvania; *State v. Valencia*, 2016, Arizona). Reasoning in these cases focused on a failure of original discretionary LWOP sentencing hearings to consider evidence of irreparable corruption and developmental immaturity as described in *Miller*.

Approaches to Achieving *Miller/Montgomery* Intent

States have fashioned various procedural approaches for meeting *Miller*'s and *Montgomery*'s requirements regarding retroactive cases. The types of developmental and clinical evidence that are relevant will be different for these various schemes. Currently there are three approaches, described in this section, used by courts to address *Miller* resentencing cases. The literature is insufficient at present to determine whether courts are trending toward a preference among these options. Examiners performing *Miller* resentencing evaluations should learn which approach prevails in the jurisdiction from which the referral is requested.

RETROSPECTIVE "LITERAL RESENTENCING" APPROACH

The retrospective resentencing approach presumes that the court must determine what sentence would have been appropriate for the individual *if, at the time of original sentencing,* Miller*'s potentially mitigating factors had been considered.* Under this approach, the focus is on the individual's developmental status and potential for rehabilitation *at the time of the original sentencing.* In his dissent in *Montgomery*, Justice Scalia presumed that the majority's decision in *Montgomery* referred to a literal resentencing (*Montgomery v. Louisiana*, 2016, p. 744), requiring the court to revisit the individual's amenability to rehabilitation and developmental status at the time of the original sentencing. One difficulty with this approach is that it could discourage taking into account a defendant's subsequent successful rehabilitation despite evidence at original sentencing that supported a finding of irreparable corruption.

PAROLE APPROACH

A few states (e.g., California, Massachusetts, Missouri) have responded to *Montgomery* by simply making all prisoners *eligible for parole consideration* if serving LWOP sentences for homicide as juveniles. Whether they should be paroled is then determined by a parole board. One appellate court's decision (*Brown v. Precythe*, 2017) aptly described most parole board deliberations as focusing on the seriousness of the offense and its implications for further offending. The court pointed out that *Montgomery* parole hearings must be different. They should apply *Miller*'s intent: for example, considering the immaturity of the inmate at the time of the offense, immaturity as it might have influenced the inmate's behavior during initial years in prison, and rehabilitation prospects. In parole hearings applying *Miller*'s perspective, clinicians may be asked to perform evaluations and offer reports for use by the parole board.

"HYBRID" APPROACH

Some resentencing courts employ an approach that considers the developmental mitigating characteristics of the individual *at the time of the offense, together with the individual's current prospects for rehabilitation.* The approach is called "hybrid" (Boone, 2015) because it combines evidence of current rehabilitation typical for parole hearings with considerations of mitigating characteristics of youthfulness at the time of the offense, to achieve a potential adjustment of the individual's sentence. To consider current prospects for rehabilitation, this approach focuses on both the extent of rehabilitation currently evident and evidence of potential for further positive change.

Two *Miller* resentencing cases exemplify this hybrid approach, as well as the relatively greater importance of current rehabilitation potential in resentencing cases. In *U.S. v. Briones* (2019), the Ninth Circuit held that the lower resentencing court had focused too much on the developmental evidence and circumstances at original sentencing and not enough on the individual's encouraging record of rehabilitation during his subsequent 20-year incarceration. The *Briones* court noted: "When a substantial delay occurs between a defendant's initial crime and later [re]sentencing, the defendant's post-incarceration conduct is especially pertinent to a *Miller* analysis" (p. 19). In *State v. Ragland* (2013), the Iowa State Supreme Court held as acceptable the lower court's ***minimal*** attention to the individual's developmental characteristics at the time of the offense while focusing more on evidence regarding the individual's record since that time as it related to rehabilitation potential. (See also *People v. Lozano*, 2016.)

Conclusion

This chapter has provided an overview of the law's recent decisions in *Miller* and *Montgomery* for criminal court sentencing of persons adjudicated for serious offenses committed as juveniles. It offered basic legal background needed by experts who perform evaluations in these cases. We defined *Miller* evaluations broadly as developmentally relevant investigations applicable to (a) juveniles facing potential LWOP, *de facto* life, and/or other criminal court sentences and (b) the resentencing of adults who have been serving LWOP sentences for homicides committed when they were adolescents. Subsequent chapters describe relevant forensic developmental concepts (Chapter 2), developmental and clinical research (Chapter 3), and evaluation procedures (Chapters 4 through 7) for *Miller* evaluations.

Compared to other types of forensic evaluations, the law associated with *Miller* sentencing and resentencing is relatively new. Some legal issues are unsettled and undergoing substantial evolution. In this context, forensic mental health examiners currently providing evaluations for *Miller* sentencing and resentencing cases are pioneers. And like all pioneers, they are especially vulnerable because of the unfamiliarity of the terrain and its demands. As in any area of forensic evaluation, *Miller* examiners must continuously research new developments in the law in this area, allowing them to adjust to changing demands. They should also be cognizant that, in their choices of ways to respond to evolving legal standards in this area, they are producing potential models for best practices of the future.

Forensic Developmental Concepts

2

The U.S. Supreme Court in *Miller* used evidence from developmental research in two ways. It identified adolescents as a group of defendants presumed less mature than adults and, therefore, less culpable for offenses; as such, they are entitled to special consideration at sentencing. The Court described five developmental features of adolescence that it used to characterize their lesser maturity. Then it ruled that these features should be weighed individually, case by case, when considering potential mitigation in sentencing or resentencing. These features, reviewed in Chapter 1, have come to be called the *Miller* factors. In addition, the Court constructed a concept called irreparable corruption to identify the rare youth who may be eligible for sentencing to life without parole (LWOP).

The Court did not define specifically how these legal concepts—irreparable corruption and the five *Miller* factors—were to be applied in judicial decision making, nor the type of forensic developmental evidence that would assist courts in these determinations. This chapter offers a logical translation of *Miller*'s legal concepts into "psycholegal" constructs (Grisso, 2013) that potentially can be assessed by forensic examiners. This analysis does not claim that all the *Miller*-related constructs can necessarily be assessed reliably. The prospects for their assessment are examined in Chapter 3, which describes what we know about potential assessment methods related to the constructs described in the present chapter.

The present chapter examines each of the five *Miller* factors in turn, followed by a section on concepts potentially relevant for irreparable corruption. Then, after a section considering the role of risk of recidivism in *Miller* cases, we describe some basic principles of child development that can guide examiners' reasoning related to various *Miller* issues.

Constructs Related to *Miller's* Decisional Immaturity Factor

Miller's first developmental factor focused on the propensity for juveniles' decisions and actions to reflect immature "recklessness, impulsivity and heedless risk-taking" (*Miller v. Alabama*, 2012, p. 2458). The Court commented also on youths' lesser autonomy in decision making—that is, greater susceptibility to influence by others, especially peers, when making choices related to their offending.

As we will describe in Chapter 3, neuroimaging of brain development and behavioral studies of youths' risk-taking behavior provide ways to conceptualize *Miller*'s decisional factor (for reviews see Scott & Steinberg, 2008; Steinberg, 2004, 2008; Steinberg & Scott, 2003). This section describes relevant constructs based on that research: (a) definitions of decision making and judgment; (b) developmental maturation of cognitive and intellectual capacities; (c) emotional and psychosocial characteristics and abilities for self-control; and (d) a concept called the "maturity gap" that is useful in framing adolescents' immature risk taking and impulsivity in making choices. Psychopathology also is of conceptual importance when considering youths' decisional immaturity in individual cases, as discussed further in research reviews in Chapter 3.

Defining Decision Making and Judgment

Miller's decisional factor focuses on the possible effects of immaturity on the process of a youth's choice to execute an act that resulted in harm to others. The terms "decision making" and "judgment" often are used to refer to the process of choice leading to an action. Decision making is the broader term, referring to any cognitive process resulting in a choice to act in situations involving options. Judgment tends to refer more specifically to the quality of discernment that was involved in the decisional process—for example, whether the individual properly weighed the options and consequences.

Decision making and judgment are influenced by many variables. Among them are (a) cognitive abilities, (b) capacities to deliberate and delay impulse, (c) the effect of cognitive heuristics (e.g., Kahneman, 2013), and (d) the context in which the decision is made. Regarding the context, some decisional situations offer time and circumstances for careful deliberation, while others demand more immediate responses under stress (often called "cold" and "hot" decision-making situations).

Cognitive and Intellectual Development

Both decision making and judgment are influenced in part by cognitive and intellectual capacities. It is well known that cognitive abilities (as measured by intelligence tests) continue to mature until they reach one's adult capacity about ages 16 to 18 on average (Icenogle et al., 2019). Individually, youths at any age differ in their level of intellectual capacity, in the degree of ability they will attain at maturity, and in the age at which they achieve it.

Useful for framing questions of cognitive maturity are Piaget's stages of cognitive development (Piaget & Inhelder, 1955). For example, cognitive development proceeds from the concrete operations stage in the first decade of life to the capacity for formal operations, which begins to emerge in the early teens and continues to develop through adolescence. However, youth with intellectual disabilities, as well as some youth with mental disorders, may struggle with abstract thinking even when they reach their adult years. Achieving the ability to engage in formal operations can have special implications in some *Miller* maturity analyses. The ability to engage in formal operations allows the individual to think in terms of abstract concepts, which is important for hypothetical and deductive reasoning—thinking in "what-if" terms, a part of the judgment process in deciding how to respond to a situation. Development of the capacity for abstract thinking also has implications for a youth's ability to imagine the impact of his or her own potential actions on other people.

Psychosocial Developmental Constructs

The mere fact of "intelligence," or having reached one's cognitive capacity, does not ensure an adult capacity for decision making and judgment. Decisions depend not only on cognitive capacity, but also on psychosocial development—the degree of maturity in emotional and social factors that influence decision making. Included in psychosocial capacities, for example, are non-cognitive capacities for self-restraint and reflection, which allow one to deliberate about the consequences of a decision before acting. Evidence offered in Chapter 3 indicates that youths mature in psychosocial capacities at a slower rate than cognitive capacities, taking longer to reach their adult maturity (for example, into the early or mid-20s). Psychosocial immaturity often makes youths' judgment less mature, less effective, and more risk taking on average than that of adults.

Psychology offers many ways to structure our thinking about psychosocial development during adolescence (e.g., Erikson, 1993; Greenberger & Sorenson, 1974). Here we describe two models of psychosocial maturity that have been offered specifically to address immaturity in adolescents' decision making and judgment related to offending. (For a detailed review, see Salekin et al., 2016.)

STEINBERG AND CAUFFMAN'S MODEL

Steinberg and Cauffman (1996; Steinberg, 2014) reviewed past developmental studies of decision making in adolescence to arrive at a model that includes three psychosocial qualities (constructs) useful for describing adolescents' relative immaturity of judgment. The model has been usefully applied in many research studies since the concepts were developed (as described in Chapter 3), as have their operational definitions and associated psychological tools to assess them. Their model has three components: responsibility, temperance, and perspective.

Responsibility refers to the development of healthy autonomy, self-reliance, and clarity of identity, so that judgment is more supported by personal reflection and less by what others would want (e.g., peers, adult authorities). Temperance refers to one's ability to limit or delay impulsive responding to situations, moderating the effects of stress on decision making, and taking time to evaluate a situation before responding. Perspective pertains to the propensity to frame problems within a larger context, taking both short-range and long-range consequences of decision options into account, and considering the impact of one's potential decision on others.

SALEKIN'S MODEL

Salekin et al. (2001, 2002) developed a three-concept model similar in some respects to Steinberg and Cauffman's. Salekin et al. used an empirical method to arrive at their classification. Their studies involved juvenile justice professionals' perceptions of adolescent offenders about whom they make legal and clinical decisions, seeking latent concepts in their consideration of young offenders' maturity and immaturity. Their model has three components: autonomy, cognitive capacities, and emotional skills.

Autonomy is somewhat like Steinberg and Cauffman's responsibility, focusing on a self-driven confidence and reflection on personal goals, resistance to pressure from others, and internal locus of control. The "cognitive capacities" component refers to abstract thinking abilities, future time perspective, grasping interpersonal relations as they relate to decision making, and capacity to do cost/benefit analyses. The "emotional skills" component (somewhat like temperance) includes abilities to manage one's feelings, to delay gratification, and to control impulses during decision making.

The "Maturity Gap" and "Dual Systems" Concepts

Two concepts have been developed to frame the way in which adolescents' decision making is less mature on average than that of adults. The maturity gap refers to the difference between cognitive and psychosocial development as just described (see, e.g., Icenogle et al., 2019). Even though adolescents' intellectual abilities begin to reach their adult capacities at around 16, psychosocial development lags throughout adolescence until reaching adult maturity in the early 20s. The difference between the growth pattern of cognitive and psychosocial development is the so-called maturity gap, explaining differences in adult and adolescent decision making even as cognitive capacities begin to match one's adult potential.

The second concept, called the dual systems model (Steinberg, 2010), frames a developmental explanation for youths' lesser psychosocial maturity. It is based on research regarding two brain-behavior maturation processes related to decision making that are ongoing throughout the second decade of life. Both processes are anchored in neuroimaging science as well as behavioral science, as described in Chapter 3. One developmental process involves a gradual increase in youths' capacities for self-regulation, which improves gradually across adolescence into the mid-20s. This involves abilities to regulate emotions, to delay impulses and promote planning, and to monitor one's own decision-making process. The second maturational process involves an increase in responsiveness to reward opportunities in the early and middle teen years. This creates a tendency for greater emotional arousal when faced with reward or threats, and a greater impulse to respond. This component begins to surge early in adolescence (around puberty), peaks in mid-adolescence, then subsides in the late teens.

These two systems develop at different rates. Maturation of self-regulatory abilities increases steadily across adolescence into the early 20s, while the second process, stimulating more impulsive decisions, surges in early adolescence and subsides in late adolescence. Thus, this second system more often overrides the capacities of the first during mid- to late adolescence, producing a greater risk for poor judgment. The risk gradually reduces as the self-regulatory system matures and as impulsive arousal by potential rewards decreases, sometime in the late teens or early 20s. These descriptions, of course, are "on average," and may vary from one youth to another depending on other factors.

The actual impact of the maturity gap and dual systems model on decision making in adolescence may be different in various real-world contexts involving what have been called "cold" and "hot" situations (Icenogle et al., 2019; Steinberg et al., 2009). Adolescents' decision-making capacities often are sufficient to produce decisions not unlike those of adults in low-stress, controlled circumstances that offer time and assistance for information processing, but far less like adults' decisions in high-stress, emotion-laden situations requiring a quick decision.

Constructs Related to *Miller*'s Dependence on Family and Environment Factor

The *Miller* decision noted that "Children are more vulnerable to negative influences and outside pressures, including from their family and peers; they have limited control over their own environment and lack the ability to extricate themselves from horrific, crime-producing settings" (*Miller v. Alabama*, 2012, p. 2458). In addition, *Miller* instructed courts to "take into account the family and home environment that surrounds him—and from which he cannot extricate himself—no matter how brutal or dysfunctional" (p. 2458). *Miller*'s focus for this factor, then, was on adverse family and environment conditions that youth cannot avoid because of their age-related dependency or their legal status as adolescents. Often youth are prohibited—legally, usually economically, and often psychologically—from "extricating" themselves (e.g., running away, disobeying authority, seeking independence) to relieve conditions that are damaging them.

The mere fact of adverse conditions in a youth's childhood is not sufficient in itself to invoke *Miller*'s dependency factor. The adverse conditions of childhood must have some potential for increasing the likelihood of criminal behavior (thus offering potential mitigation for the behavior). They might do this in various ways. For example, a family's residence in a crime-producing neighborhood might increase exposure to peer-related offending and thus the youth's own offending, or it might increase the likelihood of traumatizing experiences with implications for later offending. Family abuse and neglect, or neglect due to poverty, might contribute to mental disorders that increase the risk of offending, or they might delay development in decision-making capacities described earlier regarding psychosocial development.

Certain constructs in psychology and criminology may serve to structure evidence for these conditions. They include (a) psychological disorders with potential etiologies related to childhood abuse, neglect, or social disadvantage and (b) psychological dependency as an individual difference among adolescents.

Adverse Conditions and Psychological Development

Adverse childhood experiences (as a victim or witness of violence or psychological abuse) are frequent among youthful offenders (Baglivio et al., 2014). Not all adverse conditions of childhood have lasting consequences for a youth's development. But often they contribute to behavioral health disorders (e.g., anxiety, depression, substance abuse, and trauma- and stress-related disorders) that can interfere with normal cognitive and psychosocial decision-making development (relevant research discussed in Chapter 3). Thus, psychological concepts related to adverse conditions of childhood can play a significant role in defining *Miller*'s reference to damaging conditions for which youths "lack the ability to extricate themselves."

Some youth exposed to adverse conditions develop symptoms specific to the Trauma- and Stressor-Related Disorders described in the American Psychiatric Association's *Diagnostic and Statistical Manual of Mental Disorders* (DSM-5; American Psychiatric Association, 2013). Symptoms of Post-Traumatic Stress Disorder (PTSD) offer especially important criminogenic possibilities related to *Miller*'s dependency factor (for a review, see Zelechoski, 2016; for relevant symptoms, American Psychiatric Association, 2013, pp. 271–272). Consequences of PTSD often include a person's hypervigilance to possible danger and misinterpretation of events as threatening, as well as impulsive recklessness in responding to them. Irritability associated with PTSD can be interpreted by others as anger that provokes their own response and the individual's counter-response. Developmental delays in psychosocial development are also possible secondary effects of such disorders.

Individual Differences in Psychosocial Dependency

Miller's reference to "limited control" over one's life could be interpreted also as a question of youths' individual differences in psychosocial autonomy. Did this youth differ from age peers in his or her capacity to "extricate" himself from adverse conditions of adolescence? If so, degree of autonomy becomes a potential dimension within the dependency analysis. This capacity certainly varies with age. Yet, for adolescents at any age, there are individual differences in their own degree of psychosocial independence, assertiveness, and autonomy. Referring to the earlier discussion of the decisional factor, Salekin's autonomy and Steinberg and Cauffman's responsibility components of psychosocial maturity may provide some conceptual structure for this aspect of the dependency factor.

Constructs Related to *Miller*'s Offense Context Factor

The *Miller* offense context factor calls for consideration of "the circumstances of the homicide offense, including the extent of his participation in the conduct and the way familial and peer pressures may have affected him" (*Miller v. Alabama*, 2012, p. 2468). The Court seemed to anticipate a sentencing court's detailed examination of the offense itself—for example, what led up to the event, all that transpired during the event, and the details of the youth's participation in it. Then, using what is known about the youth's decisional, dependency, and other psychological characteristics at the time of the offense, a sentencing court would consider how the youth's characteristics—in that context—might or might not offer mitigation regarding the youth's participation in the offense.

Miller's purpose for this offense analysis does not put the focus on the heinousness of the offense (*Montgomery v. Louisiana*, 2016, p. 736) or on potential for mitigation simply because the youth was "immature." The court will want to hear the specific relation between the youth's characteristics and the offense. The offense context analysis will bear some similarity to inferential processes typically applied by courts and forensic clinicians in cases involving questions of criminal responsibility (e.g., when considering an insanity defense). Those processes examine the potential connection between an individual's psychological condition and the offense event. This conceptual process has been described for insanity cases (e.g., Melton et al., 2018; Packer, 2009) and for hearings on transfer of juveniles to criminal court (Grisso, 2013). Kinscherff (2016) also has provided helpful guidance for examining the degree to which a youth's needs and psychopathology were related to the youth's offense. When translated, these sources offer the following basic guidance for the logic process in *Miller* offense context analyses.

First, evidence must be offered that specifically and logically connects the psychological condition with the offense context. The mere presence of a mental condition at the time of the offense is not sufficient to establish a causal connection regarding the person's actions. Similarly, knowledge of a youth's psychosocial immaturity (e.g., related to the youth's status on the decisional or dependency factors) at the time of the offense does not mean that this condition necessarily influenced or accounted for the youth's judgment or the act itself. Psychosocial immaturity may be a predicate for the question, but some logical connection to the offense event must be shown.

Second, alternative hypotheses about the relation of the youth's characteristic to the offense must be examined and weighed. Merely finding a plausible logical connection is insufficient. As with all analyses guided by scientific logic, one must generate and consider alternative hypotheses about the relation of a youth's immaturity to the event (including no relation), not merely examine the hypothesis that seems plausible initially.

Third, one must weigh the strength of the available evidence for each of the alternatives in search of the most plausible one. An important part of this process is an active search for data that might contradict each of the hypotheses.

Constructs Related to *Miller's* Prospects for Rehabilitation Factor

Miller noted that "A child's character is not as well formed as an adult's; his traits are less fixed" (*Miller v. Alabama*, 2012, p. 2458), which requires adequate consideration of "a child's capacity for change" (p. 2465). The Court also referred to scientific evidence that most youth with delinquency records do not continue their offending into adulthood, but instead desist as they mature beyond adolescence. When determining an alternative sentence to LWOP, therefore, the *Miller* prospects for rehabilitation factor requires an inquiry into the potential for remediation. Because *Miller* sentencing defendants will eventually receive very long sentences, the time frame for considering potential for change is long. The time frames in some *Miller* resentencing cases can be shorter (especially when parole is being considered); in this situation, the individual's past rehabilitation progress during the prison term will be examined as an indicator of potential for future change.

In the justice system context, the objective of rehabilitation is positive growth to reduce future offending risk and enhance one's capacity for a productive life. Courts often use the words "rehabilitation" and "treatment" interchangeably when referring to this objective, but Kinscherff (2016) suggested that they should be distinguished. Rehabilitation is best seen as the general objective of justice system intervention and the full range of methods aimed at that objective (as discussed later). In contrast, treatment refers to the narrower clinical objective to reduce symptoms of psychopathological conditions (e.g., disorders or disabilities) and interventions (e.g., psychopharmacologic, psychotherapeutic) to further that objective.

Conceptualizing Prospects for Rehabilitation

The assessment of prospects for rehabilitation of juvenile offenders has been conceptualized as involving the evaluation of two components (Grisso, 2013; Heilbrun et al., 2017; *Kent v. U.S.*, 1966; Kinscherff, 2016; Larson & Grisso, 2016; Melton et al., 2018). The first is the characteristics of the individual that may require rehabilitation and the characteristics that might promote or complicate successful outcomes. In the following discussion we refer to this as the "amenability" component—that is, the youth's amenability to rehabilitative change. The second component is the nature, dosage, quality, and existence of interventions that are appropriate for that youth, which we call the "appropriate interventions" component.

The two components contribute to a "person-environment" approach to framing the question of "prospects," defining it as dependent on both the youth's qualities and the appropriateness and qualities of the interventions. These two concepts are similar to what has been conceptualized, respectively, as "specific responsivity" (characteristics of the youth that should be considered shaping intervention plans) and "general responsivity" (characteristics inherent in the intervention itself) (Andrews & Bonta, 2017).

Examiners in the past have used these two concepts together in juvenile court sentencing (disposition) cases and in transfer (waiver) cases. However, the *Miller* examiner should be aware that the purpose of a prospects for rehabilitation analysis in *Miller* sentencing cases is fundamentally different from its purpose in juvenile court cases. In juvenile court disposition cases, the rehabilitation question focuses on constructing a rehabilitation plan designed to meet the youth's needs and reduce recidivism, as well as estimating its likelihood of succeeding (Grisso, 2013). In transfer (waiver) cases, the question focuses on whether the youth can be rehabilitated with services provided by the juvenile justice system within the time frame of that jurisdiction.

In contrast, *Miller* sentencing does not seek to identify rehabilitation methods that are best suited for the youth's rehabilitation. It asks whether something less than LWOP is warranted, given the defendant's degree of immaturity and potential malleability. Moreover, unlike juvenile justice objectives, the nature of *Miller* sentencing if LWOP is rejected virtually guarantees that youths will receive long prison sentences that often will not be designed to provide rehabilitation services tailored to their developmental needs.

Therefore, the purpose of prospects for rehabilitation in *Miller* sentencing cases is not, as in juvenile court dispositions, to describe what services could best promote positive change in the youth. The purpose is to offer the court information that speaks to the mitigating possibility that the characteristics of the youth suggest potential for change. Framed in this way, the two components used to shape prospects for rehabilitation in *Miller* cases will receive different emphases than in juvenile disposition cases. The focus primarily will be on the amenability of the youth—describing characteristics of the youth that make rehabilitation and change more or less likely. The appropriate interventions component will receive less attention, given the realistic limitations of constructing a "treatment plan" for the individual within the context of a lengthy prison sentence.

Notwithstanding this difference, we suggest that *Miller* examiners should include both the amenability and appropriate interventions components in their framework for thinking about factors relevant for *Miller*'s prospects for rehabilitation factor. The reasons for this will become clear later in this discussion.

The Amenability Component

Grisso (2015) has suggested that there are two parts to the amenability question: (a) characteristics of the individual that are contributing to offending and therefore are in need of change and (b) the individual's characteristics that may be relevant for the person's response to rehabilitation. There have been efforts to create ways to conceptualize these aspects of amenability.

CHARACTERISTICS CONTRIBUTING TO OFFENDING

Part of the analysis of potential for change is identification of the characteristics or circumstances of the individual that would require change to promote rehabilitation and reduce offending (Grisso, 2013). These are sometimes called "criminogenic" factors: that is, features of personality, behavioral health, or the person's social circumstances that have been contributing to the individual's offending. For the *Miller* sentencing examiner, this involves identifying the factors in this individual case that are most salient for explaining the defendant's past offending and the present adjudicated offense. The nature and severity of these factors often are important in an analysis of prospects for rehabilitation.

In the context of *Miller* sentencing cases, the most fundamental concepts for describing what has contributed to a youth's past offending often are those pertaining to adolescent development. As described in the earlier discussions of the decisional and dependency *Miller* factors, a developmental model offers explanations for youths' offending related, at least in part, to decisional and psychosocial immaturity and dependency. Thus, any analysis of contributors to youths' past offending and/or the adjudicated offense must focus on those concepts provided by a developmental perspective.

Conceptual frameworks have been provided for considering broader social and cultural interactions and youths' development. The impact of racial discrimination throughout a youth's development is often necessary to consider when examining factors contributing to a youth's offending related to *Miller*'s dependency factor (e.g., Benner et al., 2018). In addition, socioeconomic disadvantage can affect neurological brain development, with implications for capacities related to *Miller*'s decisional factor (e.g., Buckley et al., 2019).

In addition, several ways to conceptualize and classify potential criminogenic factors have been developed, of which two will be offered here. Hoge (2016) describes eight criminogenic factors developed for use within the Risk-Needs-Responsivity (RNR) model applied to juveniles (see also Arnold et al., 2018):

- History of Conduct Disorder or criminal activity
- Dysfunctional parenting
- Educational or employment deficiencies
- Antisocial peer associations
- Substance abuse
- Poor use of leisure time
- Personality or behavior dysfunction (e.g., mental disorders, trauma)
- Antisocial attitudes, values and beliefs

A lengthier set of criminogenic factors has been provided by a Department of Justice project based on extensive review of major studies on risk factors for offending (for the list and a review, see Cunningham, 2010). This is applicable for adults but should be used cautiously with juveniles.

INDIVIDUAL CHARACTERISTICS RELATED TO REHABILITATION RESPONSE

In the context of *Miller* sentencing, an important concept for describing a youth's potential for change is the concept of maturation. Research reviewed in Chapter 3 supports the assumption that change is normative as young people develop from adolescence into their mid-20s. In addition, their capacity for change increases as they age into adulthood and acquire greater psychosocial maturity. Classifying a youth according to developmental norms is an integral part of understanding the youth's potential to respond to future rehabilitative efforts.

In addition, the literature offers three models for organizing a youth's characteristics that might promote or inhibit rehabilitative change. First, Salekin's (2015) model includes several individual characteristics associated with greater or lesser potential for change. His approach was based in part on factor-analytic survey research with forensic mental health professionals (Salekin et al., 2001) and juvenile court judges (Salekin et al., 2002) to examine their implicit meanings of amenability. Salekin's model involves three domains: (a) psychopathology: degree and type (e.g., mental disorders and disabilities that may offer more or less resistance to change); (b) responsibility and motivation to change (e.g., open to influence, assumption of responsibility, experiences sufficient discomfort to motivate participation in rehabilitation efforts); and (c) consideration and tolerance of others (e.g., capacity for empathy, social responsiveness).

Second, Grisso (2013) offered an analysis of a youth's potential for change based on a consideration of factors identified more broadly in literature on psychotherapy and patient readiness. He suggested three characteristics relevant for receptiveness to intervention: (a) the youth's degree of discomfort with his or her own behavior and life situation; (b) the youth's potential for social attachments; and (c) the chronicity of the youth's illegal behavior and conditions that may be influencing it.

Third, Hoge (2016) describes the concept of "responsivity" (within the RNR model). It offers various factors to consider when evaluating a youth's or adult's potential responsiveness to rehabilitation efforts. The concept focuses on characteristics of the individual or the individual's situation (e.g., family) that might complicate rehabilitation efforts, but also strengths of the individual that might promote positive change (see also Andrews & Bonta, 2017; DeMatteo et al., 2016).

The Appropriate Interventions Component

The appropriate interventions component in an interactive analysis of prospect for rehabilitation focuses on potential interventions appropriate for the individual. The *Miller* context in which a consideration of appropriate interventions will be most salient is *Miller* resentencing cases, especially those that involve parole potential. However, considering appropriate interventions for the future is conceptually less relevant for youths in *Miller* sentencing cases, for the following reasons.

All that we know conceptually (and empirically: see Chapter 3) about appropriate rehabilitation methods for juveniles is based on services within the juvenile justice system, or available to it in the community. Whether those services would be appropriate for a given youth is irrelevant in *Miller* sentencing cases, because typically they will not be available. *Miller* sentencing defendants typically face long sentences in adult prisons in which services are limited and are unlike those conceptually designed for juveniles. We know little conceptually or empirically about adolescents' (or emerging adults') prospects for rehabilitation within prison programs that are not designed for them.

Nevertheless, *Miller* examiners should be aware of ways to conceptualize appropriate interventions both in juvenile justice and adult correctional settings, as well as in community-based services. As noted earlier, the component may be of value in resentencing cases (especially where parole is possible), and occasionally in

Miller sentencing cases in which a beneficial service known to exist in prison would match a youth's responsivity. In addition, as noted later, appropriate interventions concepts may be helpful in explaining lack of past responsiveness to rehabilitation efforts.

Available interventions in adult correctional settings may vary greatly within and across these settings. In general, however, they can be grouped as three broad categories (Duwe, 2017): (a) educational and employability interventions (e.g., formal education, skill development associated with occupations); (b) cognitive restructuring interventions (e.g., social skills training, anger management, substance use reduction, psychopathy-focused interventions); and (c) health, psychiatric, and psychology-based interventions (e.g., psychopharmacological services, psychotherapeutic interventions for diagnostic conditions such as trauma and depression).

Modern efforts to improve rehabilitation interventions in both juvenile justice and criminal justice have supported the importance of three concepts to consider when weighing the potential of interventions to contribute to an individual's rehabilitation. The first is intervention matching (or treatment matching), which emphasizes that an intervention is more often successful when properly matched with the needs and characteristics of the person (e.g., Andrews & Bobta, 2017; Vieira et al., 2009). The concept extends beyond mode of intervention to such matters as individual differences in necessary dosage (intensity of the intervention) and length of time the intervention is applied.

The second concept, evidence-based practice, focuses on the quality of modes of intervention, which varies greatly (Lipsey, 2009). Evidence-based methods are those with adequate research to have demonstrated their rehabilitative value. Third, even evidence-based interventions vary in the fidelity with which they are applied in specific programs and settings (Cruise et al., 2016; Lipsey, 2009). Sometimes interventions are applied in ways that do not conform to the standardized (manualized) conditions for which they were validated, due to negligence, intentional non-validated modifications, or deficiencies in training of those providing the intervention (Duwe & Clark, 2015). A combination of poor intervention matching and lack of fidelity can occur when interventions are used with individuals with demographic characteristics (e.g., age, gender, race/ethnicity) or diagnostic features (e.g., mental disorders, psychopathy) for whom the intervention was not intended or was not validated.

These three concepts (intervention matching, evidence-based practice, and fidelity) can play an important role when examining apparent lack of rehabilitation success in juvenile justice or prison interventions provided to the defendant in the past. Such failures might be due to lack of amenability. Often, however, they are due to a mismatch between the individual's needs and the type of intervention, or to deficiencies in the quality of its implementation.

Constructs Related to *Miller*'s Legal Competency Factor

Miller recognized that mandatory sentencing "ignores that he might have been charged and convicted of a lesser offense if not for incompetencies associated with youth—for example, his inability to deal with police officers or prosecutors (including a plea agreement) or his incapacity to assist his own attorneys" (*Miller v. Alabama*, 2012, p. 2468, citing *Graham*). The Court's concern was with youths' immaturity that might create a disadvantage during the adjudicative process, potentially placing them in the position of eligibility for a lengthy sentence they might not otherwise have faced.

The legal competency factor offers a different type of mitigation than the other *Miller* factors. It pertains not to the effects of immaturity on juveniles' offending or rehabilitation, but to potential developmentally related procedural errors that may have led to their conviction. Examples include immature responses to police interrogation, or immature capacities for competence to stand trial. Nothing in *Miller* or *Montgomery* suggests that courts are expected to revisit those potential due process errors in a *Miller* sentencing or resentencing cases, and, in our experience, it happens only rarely.

For this reason, at present the legal competency factor is best viewed as one of the U.S. Supreme Court's justifications for identifying juveniles as a special class deserving of mitigation in sentencing, but not as a factor requiring judicial consideration or forensic evaluations in the *Miller* sentencing context (Grisso & Kavanaugh, 2016; Scott et al., 2016). If this assumption proves wrong in future cases, courts and forensic examiners can look to numerous developmentally relevant constructs for framing questions of youths' legal competencies (e.g., Grisso, 2005; Kassin et al., 2010; Kruh & Grisso, 2009; Richardson et al., 1995).

Constructs Related to Irreparable Corruption

Miller concluded that an LWOP sentence could not be given in juvenile homicide cases unless the youth was irreparably corrupt. The Court's discussion did not specifically define the criteria for this legal concept, and the Court did not require a specific finding. However, it allowed LWOP only for the irreparably corrupt youth. Moreover, the condition was identified in two ways. First, it was described as extremely rare. The Court presumed only the rarest of *Miller* defendants would meet the criterion, based on research regarding adolescents' strong tendency toward desistance from crime as they mature (see evidence in Chapter 3). Second, the Court used several terms to label the construct: permanent and irreparable "corruption," "depravity," and "incorrigibility."

On their face, these labels suggest that it requires a psychological condition that must be criminogenic in nature—that is, a source of past and future criminal behavior. Moreover, the condition must be pervasive and unmodifiable. Heilbrun et al. (2017), for example, defined the legal concept as a condition that "cannot be rehabilitated by maturation or by psychological-behavioral interventions" (p. 46; logically, also not by biological or psychopharmacological interventions). In sum, as described in Chapter 1, the Court's discussion of the concept strongly suggests that irreparable corruption is (a) a condition (corruption, depravity, or incorrigibility) that (b) promotes lifetime offending and (c) cannot be changed (irreparable, permanent, or irretrievable) (d) by any means (e.g., punishment, therapeutic intervention, education, or maturation).

It is important to recognize some questions that are not posed by the concept of irreparable corruption as we have defined it. First, the question of irreparable corruption does not ask whether rehabilitation of the individual will be difficult (which is not rare), but whether it can ever happen. Second, following *Montgomery v. Louisiana* (2016), the heinousness of the crime cannot itself be used to infer the condition of irreparable corruption ("children who commit even heinous crimes are capable of change," p. 736, citing *Roper*). Third, irreparable corruption is not addressed simply by determining that the person is very likely to reoffend. The concept requires a prediction of lifetime reoffending. Fourth, the mere fact that an offender poses a substantial risk of reoffending does not mean that the risk cannot be changed. Finally, as noted in Chapter 1, irreparable corruption is not synonymous with developmental maturity and frequent offending (see *Veal v. State*, 2016). The concept "sophistication and maturity" (discussed later) is applied in many states as a criterion in hearings on transfer of youths to criminal court (Grisso, 2013; Heilbrun et al., 2017). But maturity and frequent offending alone do not provide evidence that a person can never be changed.

Fairfax-Columbo et al. (2019) have offered a conceptual guide when considering the question of irreparable corruption, employing three logical steps. The first step uses concepts and research evidence about life-course persistence or desistence from crime as a baseline estimation of future offending. Research indicating that the great majority of youthful offenders desist from offending in young adulthood (see Chapter 3) creates a default assumption that lifetime future offending will be rare. The second step requires using psychological concepts and measures to identify characteristics of the defendant that may warrant adjusting the estimate of future criminal behavior to identify whether the defendant may be a life-course-persistent offender or one is likely (as is the norm for adolescents) to desist. The third step then examines prospects for rehabilitation as required by *Miller*.

In this section, we review several psychological and psychiatric constructs one might be inclined to consider within the logic described by Fairfax-Columbo et al. (2019) when addressing irreparable corruption: (a) life-course-persistent offending, (b) psychopathy, (c) sophistication and maturity, (d) rehabilitation potential, and (e) intractable mental or neurological conditions. Here we describe their potential as constructs related to irreparable corruption; then, Chapter 3 reviews research on these constructs and their measurement. The present review, together with Chapter 3, suggests that courts and clinicians applying this model and using the constructs we review would encounter serious difficulties in concluding that a youth is irreparably corrupt.

Life-Course-Persistent Offending

Moffit (1993, 2006) described two types of adolescent offenders. Adolescence-limited offenders desist from offending as they approach adulthood. This is consistent with the well-known age–crime curve that documents an increase in arrests across adolescence that peak around 17 to 21 and then decline markedly by age 30 and continue to further decrease thereafter (Farrington, 1986; Mulvey et al., 2004; Sampson & Loeb, 2003). Moffit's life-course-persistent (LCP) offenders (less than about 15% of young offenders) do not follow this normative age-based decline with maturation, but rather persist in their frequent offending into adulthood (Moffitt, 1993, 2006). As a small proportion of delinquent youth whose offending persists, LCP begins to identify the "territory" of the law's irreparable corruption and its presumed rarity.

Research reviewed in Chapter 3 supports the value of the LCP concept as a basis for the default assumption in Step 1 of the Fairfax-Columbo et al. model. However, it also poses several limitations when applied in Step 2. Among them are evidence that there are several LCP developmental patterns; there is not a single type of LCP youth. As we shall see in Chapter 3, there are also difficulties in distinguishing LCP youths from adolescence-limited youths during adolescence. Finally, the LCP concept refers to continued offending into adulthood, but takes no account of potential responsiveness to interventions intended to reduce future offending. Therefore, LCP as a concept does not imply the "cannot change" component of irreparable corruption.

Moving from Step 2 to Step 3 requires the use of concepts, reviewed below, regarding the individual characteristics of the defendant, in search of adjustments regarding the likelihood of rehabilitation to identify the youth who can never be rehabilitated. What are the conceptual prospects for doing this?

Psychopathy

Psychopathy is a personality construct that, in adults, includes interpersonal characteristics (e.g., manipulative, deceitful), affective characteristics (e.g., callous, unemotional, lack of empathy), and antisocial behavioral characteristics that increase the risk of chronic criminal offending (Cleckley, 1976; Hart, 1998; Vincent & Hart, 2012). The affective component, often labeled "callous-unemotional" (CU), is considered the most basic and most identifiable characteristic among adolescents who later develop psychopathy in adulthood (Vincent et al., 2016). Some of psychopathy's CU features are included in the DSM-5's diagnoses of Conduct Disorder in persons below age 18 and in Antisocial Personality Disorder at age 18 and older (American Psychiatric Association, 2013). CU traits are not required for these diagnoses but are among the contributing factors. Psychopathy in adults and the concept of CU traits in adolescents have been useful for describing an especially difficult group of young offenders regarding prospects for rehabilitation (for a review applicable to adolescents, see Frick & White, 2008). The conditions are presumed to be chronic, persistent, and difficult to change by current psychological interventions.

Psychopathy, therefore, includes features that address irreparable corruption's concerns for traits that are criminogenic and difficult to change. If a defendant were identified as only moderate or low on the psychopathy or CU continuum, logically this would weigh against irreparable corruption. Finding a youth high in CU traits would raise the question of difficulty in modification. Yet, there are conceptual and practical limitations to inferring that this is a sign that the youth would be psychopathic in adulthood or that the youth could never be rehabilitated. Such a claim would require evidence that the condition (a) can be reliably identified during adolescence, (b) is stable (will endure well into adulthood), and (c) cannot be changed.

Chapter 3 offers research evidence contrary to these three assumptions. In brief, research indicates that most adults who manifest psychopathy have displayed high CU traits in adolescence, but most adolescents with apparent CU traits do not manifest psychopathy in adulthood. Moreover, research described in Chapter 3 supports the conclusion that psychopathic and CU traits offer greater resistance to rehabilitation, but not that they can never be modified.

Sophistication and Maturity

"Sophistication and maturity," a legal and forensic concept applied to adolescent offenders, is a legacy of *Kent v. U.S.* (1966) and its criteria for transfer (waiver) to criminal court (Grisso, 2013; Heilbrun et al., 2017). Its precise meaning, however, has been difficult to pin down. Salekin et al. (2002) found diverse meanings in a study of juvenile court judges' own definitions. They included (a) criminal sophistication (criminal behavior as a way of life); (b) culpability (sufficiently mature to form criminal intent); (c) social maturity (sufficiently mature to understand social norms); and (d) cognitive maturity (capacity to delay impulses).

Reviewing these various meanings of the concept, Salekin et al. (2016) offered a construct of "sophistication and maturity" including three components. First, the youth is mature psychologically—for example, advanced in abilities to consider consequences, manage self-control, and make careful independent judgments. Second, the youth is criminally sophisticated in the sense of consistently employing his or her maturity in antisocial ways. Third, the youth has a criminal identity manifested by well-formed criminal thinking, similar to traits associated with psychopathy.

Any consideration of the relevance of this concept to irreparable corruption would require that the youth be extremely high on all three of its components. Even then, however, the concept as Salekin et al. describe it does not imply an irreparable condition but, like psychopathy, leads one to infer greater challenges to its modification. Moreover, as noted in Chapter 3, currently there are no studies of the relation between measures of "sophistication and maturity" in adolescence and their lifetime relation to offending and rehabilitation potential.

Rehabilitation Potential

Earlier we reviewed concepts related to amenability in a section on *Miller*'s prospects for rehabilitation factor. Logically, the "irreparable" nature of irreparable corruption suggests the relevance of all those concepts and data for the irreparable corruption analysis. In that discussion, we reviewed concepts including the use of a developmental model of normative change, concepts for identifying personal characteristics regarding receptivity to change, and concepts related to criminogenic factors contributing to the individual's offending.

Intractable Mental and Neurological Conditions

Some *Miller* cases may involve the presence of a psychological, psychiatric, or neurological condition responsible for an individual's criminal behavior that cannot be altered with treatment. Examples include profound intellectual disability, certain cases of chronic psychosis, or behavioral dysregulation due to neurological trauma (permanent brain damage).

None of these conditions is always (or even usually) irreparable or without prospect for means to compensate for the person's disability. Thus, their mere presence would not offer a parallel concept to irreparable corruption. However, in individual cases, if one of the conditions is identified as unalterable by any known means, and if it can be demonstrated that the condition is (in this case) responsible for the person's past and continued criminal behavior, the condition would be conceptually relevant for considering irreparable corruption in that specific case.

One might argue that another condition potentially rendering a youth "irreparable" is extreme childhood deprivation—abuse or neglect of a type that was frequent, prolonged, and unremitting. Such cases do occur. As noted in Chapter 1, however, several state courts have concluded that the logic of *Miller* does not allow damage inflicted on a youth (e.g., abuse, neglect, deprivation) to be used as an aggravating circumstance—that is, as evidence that a youth qualifies for LWOP because of irreparable corruption.

Irreparable Corruption in *Miller* Resentencing Cases

Recall from Chapter 1 that resentencing under *Montgomery* often will involve prisoners who will have been serving an LWOP sentence for many years. Usually they will be adults in their 20s or older at the time of resentencing. Some of the psychological constructs reviewed above as potentially related to irreparable corruption may have fewer limitations in some resentencing cases. For example, the application of psychopathy to adults as a construct and an object of assessment is better supported than for adolescents (although Chapter 3 offers evidence that "adults with psychopathy are untreatable" is not as accepted as it once was). Similarly, in resentencing cases involving offenders well into their adult years, risk-of-recidivism scores as well as the LCP concept may sometimes have additional value for the irreparable corruption analysis based on any reliable data concerning the individual's behavior during his or her time in prison.

Summary of Irreparable Corruption

This review of psychological and psychiatric constructs, together with research evidence examined later in Chapter 3, suggests serious limits for their application by forensic examiners to identify the irreparably corrupt youth in *Miller* sentencing cases. No psychological concept predicts a condition of lifetime criminal propensity that can never be changed in any case by any means. This conclusion both supports and limits the value of the model described earlier by Fairfax-Columbo et al. (2019). The model uses logical concepts that can assist clinicians to describe the relative (low, moderate, high) likelihood of continued offending and potential for rehabilitation, at least in the immediate future. But the concepts and the research using them do not allow for predictions that a youth will be a "lifetime risk" and "can never change." This conclusion is consistent with a statement by the American Psychological Association in its amicus brief in *Miller*, claiming that psychology has "no reliable way to determine that a juvenile's offenses are the result of an irredeemably corrupt character" (Amicus Brief for American Psychological Association et al., 2012, p. 25).

Risk of Recidivism

The term "risk assessment," as used in modern forensic assessment, refers to at least three types of risk analyses (as represented in the RNR model: Hoge, 2016). Earlier discussions of risk concepts for use in *Miller* evaluations have focused on two of these: (a) identifying criminogenic risk factors (called "Needs" in the RNR model) that have contributed to a person's offending in the past and (b) identifying responsivity factors that may complicate or promote efforts to reduce future risk of offending (called "Responsivity" in the RNR model).

Absent from previous discussion in this chapter has been the first "R" in RNR—risk of recidivism. This refers to estimates of the actual likelihood of re-offending. In modern forensic assessment, typically a risk-of-recidivism estimate is operationalized with a set of risk factors empirically tested to predict, estimate the probability, or classify as low, moderate, or high an individual's likelihood of re-offending when compared to other offenders. Chapter 3 will review some of those empirically tested methods. When is the concept and measurement of risk of recidivism appropriate for *Miller* cases?

Risk of Recidivism in *Miller* Resentencing Cases

An estimate of likelihood of future reoffending (recidivism) often will be conceptually appropriate for many *Miller* resentencing cases. This is most likely in resentencing circumstances in which the prospect of release to the community in the not-too-distant future exists. For example, some jurisdictions have implemented a parole eligibility process to satisfy *Montgomery*'s requirements (see

Chapter 1). In other cases, a once-lengthy sentence, perhaps half of which has been served, might have the potential to be significantly shortened. In both of those situations, risk-of-recidivism estimates focused on release to the community are warranted. Conceptually, they represent important information to consider in those circumstances. Empirically, risk-of-recidivism measures have been validated for community-based recidivism using follow-up periods that may exceed the individual's remaining stay in prison.

Risk of Recidivism in *Miller* Sentencing Cases

In contrast, risk of re-offending lacks relevance in *Miller* sentencing evaluations involving juveniles being sentenced in criminal court. There are several practical, conceptual, and empirical reasons for this.

First, *Miller* sentencing defendants will be receiving lengthy prison sentences. Yet, in most cases, methods for estimating risk of recidivism have been validated with offenders followed up while in the community. Since *Miller* sentencing defendants will not be in the community, on which the norms are based, a risk-of-recidivism estimate is not relevant.

Second, in cases involving judicial decisions about length of sentence, a risk-of-recidivism estimate at time of sentencing will be of no value for predicting re-offending when the *Miller* sentencing defendant is released from prison several decades later. Empirical methods offering risk estimates for youths have used follow-up periods for validation that fall far short of the times that *Miller* defendants will be serving before release (see Chapter 3). Moreover, the length of time between sentencing evaluation and future release offers a great deal of time for risk factors to change.

Third, predicting *future* offending while in prison is not likely to be a factor in the sentencing decision for *Miller* sentencing defendants. But if it were, there is no evidence that validated risk-of-recidivism estimates for youths are predictive of prison behavior, since normative validation has focused on community-based re-offending.

Fourth, estimates of risk of recidivism have little value for assessing the potential for rehabilitation or irreparable corruption.

A high level of risk of recidivism may suggest a greater need for security and/or services but does not conceptually or empirically indicate a low likelihood of rehabilitation. (For further explanation, see Grisso & Kavanaugh, 2016.)

Despite these conceptual points, *Miller* sentencing examiners might encounter circumstances in some jurisdictions that seem to require an estimate of risk of recidivism. In addition, some judges or attorneys may ask for an estimate of risk of recidivism in a *Miller* sentencing case. Examiners may decide to provide it, but the conceptual and empirical issues we have described may obligate the examiner to educate the court regarding the risk estimate's limited value.

Developmental Constructs for General Application

Addressing each of the *Miller* factors requires a sound grasp of general principles of human development and its role in psychopathology. Child development as a science conceptualizes the process of growth and maturation from birth through emerging adulthood. Most developmentalists identify three broad categories of growth and maturation: biological, cognitive or intellectual, and psychosocial. For each of these areas, developmental psychology provides theories, principles, stages, and descriptions of growth on average at various ages.

The following review describes some of the most basic and relevant developmental principles that will be useful when reasoning about issues in *Miller* cases, The review is general and does not provide specific citations for each of its assertions. Support may be found by consulting basic developmental textbooks (e.g., Lamb & Freund, 2010; Steinberg, 2017) and explanations in other resources on forensic evaluation of juveniles (e.g., Grisso, 2004, 2013).

Sequential Process of Development

Maturation proceeds in an orderly sequence within any of the three growth categories. For example, certain neurological brain structures develop before others. Cognitively, the ability to perform concrete operations occurs before youth acquire capacities for abstract thinking. Children perceive certain social behaviors as right or wrong because authorities say so, and later they gain the ability to see such things as an agreement among a society's citizens aimed at maintaining order. The predictable sequence of development extends also to interdependence between the three categories of growth. For example, certain neurological brain structures must mature before certain cognitive or psychosocial capacities evolve.

Variation in Individual Development

Developmental psychologists have described the age-related averages for various features of biological, cognitive, and psychosocial growth. Age-related averages are useful for many purposes. Yet one cannot infer a specific youth's level of functioning based simply on his or her age and normative data, because there is considerable variability in maturation within an age. Individual differences among youth may delay or accelerate their development in relation to their age-peer average. Poorer or better intellectual capacity may advance or delay development in cognitive and psychosocial abilities. Delays also may be related to the episodic effects of mental disorders on normal growth. Developmental delays may occur because of environmental differences such as exposure to inferior educational systems, conditions of poverty and neglect, and events leading to childhood or adolescent disorders (e.g., trauma).

Discontinuity in Development

Although development on average proceeds in predictable stages, individual youth often do not mature in an "orderly" fashion. This is manifested in three ways. First, they may progress at a different pace in one area of growth than another. For example, a youth may develop normally (at age-peer average) in intellectual development but be delayed or accelerated in social skills. Second, the youth's growth in a specific ability may be temporarily delayed with the possibility that it will adjust later. This may happen, for example, when the youth experiences onset of a mental disorder or trauma that arrests development temporarily, but the youth will potentially be able to "catch up" when the disorder subsides.

Third, in certain circumstances, youth may fail to exercise a capacity they have only recently achieved and that has not yet been rehearsed sufficiently to be readily available to them. This can happen, for example, when the more mature response was learned recently in a specific social situation but has not been yet generalized to apply in other situations. In stressful situations requiring a rapid response, a youth might be capable of an effective, adaptive response but, if that response was only recently learned, stress may interfere with its use in favor of a better-learned (but less mature) response.

The Meaning of "Immature" and "Mature"

In *Miller* cases, courts sometimes will ask forensic examiners whether the youth is "mature" or "immature." In contrast, from a developmental psychological perspective, there is no single definition of "maturity." For several reasons, identifying a person simply as mature or immature is not meaningful without reframing the question.

First, "immaturity" is always relative, requiring a point of comparison. A 15-year-old boy may be mature compared to younger youth or a youth his own age, but immature in relation to older adolescents or adults. *Second, a youth may be relatively mature in some ways and not others*: for example, biologically but less so socially, or cognitively but less so in psychosocial skills. *Third, society's or law's definitions of maturity often are linked to specific circumstances.* Laws define different "ages of maturity" for driving, drinking, independent decision making about certain types of medical care, joining the armed forces, voting, and auto rental. One may be legally mature for some purposes and not others. For all three of these reasons, it makes no sense (developmentally or legally) to express conclusions that a youth is simply "mature" or "immature" without qualifying the statement according to some context or point of comparison.

Developmental Perspective for Clinical Conditions

Developmental psychopathology offers principles and concepts regarding adolescents' mental disorders or disabilities that are relevant for the *Miller* factors. Adolescents' biological, psychological, and social immaturity levels influence the nature and course of psychopathology and treatment differently than for adults. These differences often are not apparent to legal professionals in adult criminal courts that hear *Miller* cases, given their lesser experience with juveniles. We refer *Miller* examiners to general texts on developmental psychopathology for reviews of the following ways in which adolescents' clinical conditions manifest differently than adult disorders (Cicchetti, 1984; Cicchetti & Rogosch, 2002; Mash & Barkley, 2014;for forensic purposes, Grisso, 2004). Three concepts for a developmental perspective on adolescents' disorders are (a) age relativity, (b) comorbidity, and (c) discontinuity of disorders.

First, regarding age relativity, mental disorders, their symptoms, and their identification vary in relation to age. Some disorders are more prevalent among youth than among adults (e.g., Attention-Deficit/Hyperactivity Disorder [ADHD]) or are less prevalent (e.g., Schizophrenia Spectrum disorders). In addition, typical symptoms of a disorder may vary with age. For example, depression in adolescence more often includes anger and irritability than among adults. Similarly, common symptoms for a disorder may be different for younger compared to older adolescents. And some behaviors are normal for children or adolescents at one age but abnormal and signs of psychopathology when manifested at an older age.

Second, comorbidity is common for those adolescents with mental disorders. In adults, mental disorders are relatively discrete, while in childhood and adolescence they are less differentiated, so that comorbidity of diagnostic conditions is more common. For example, adolescents with mood disorders often present with anxiety disorders as well. A great majority of youths diagnosed with Conduct Disorder meet criteria also for ADHD, mood disorders, and/or substance use disorders. This becomes important in *Miller* cases in which the presence of Conduct Disorder, without proper attention to comorbidity, may focus the inquiry on the youth's antisocial character without proper regard for the potential relevance of other disorders.

Finally, regarding discontinuity, youths' diagnoses at a point in time are less likely to be reliable indicators of their conditions prior to that point or for the short- or long-term future. Adolescents change more from year to year than do adults because of their continuous biological and psychological development. Their mental disorders and disabilities, therefore, may be more fluid and labile and of less certain continuity. This can be of some consequence in *Miller* cases when a diagnosis at the time of sentencing is used to infer disorders at the time of the offense or regarding future rehabilitation and treatment efforts.

Developmental Sociological Concepts

Finally, sociology and criminology have developed many constructs relevant for understanding the causes and course of delinquency. These include causal theories of delinquency and classifications of types of delinquency. They include also the research and concepts reviewed earlier in his chapter regarding age–crime curves and patterns of desistance or LCP in offending. Summaries of these developmental sociological concepts can be found in other sources (e.g., Farrington, 2008; Gottfredson, 2003; Russell & Odgers, 2016; Shoemaker, 2010), and Chapter 3 reviews research related to some of these constructs.

Conclusion

This chapter has offered a review of psychological, psychiatric, and sociological concepts relevant for application to the legal concepts in *Miller* cases—irreparable corruption and the five *Miller* factors. Use of these concepts allows one to design and implement the evaluation in a manner that enhances the legal relevance of the data obtained and their interpretation. It is important to understand that their legal relevance, however, does not literally operationalize the legal standard. No data, for example, justify a forensic clinician's expert opinion that a youth's decisional abilities are so great or so deficient as to render the youth sufficiently or insufficiently culpable, blameworthy, or deserving of a specific sentence. The forensic examiner's role is to provide the data, as well as a comparative developmental perspective on relevant maturity or immaturity, that assist a judicial decision to make that legal judgment.

Chapter 2 has offered concepts to help frame the collection and organization of data relevant for *Miller* sentencing and resentencing. Chapter 3 will examine research-based information for the use of these concepts, as well as options that are available for assessment methods in *Miller* cases.

3 Empirical Foundations and Limits

Best practices in forensic mental health evaluations require evidence from the behavioral, social, and medical sciences for their empirical foundation (Heilbrun et al., 2009). This applies to the reliability and validity of forensic examiners' data collection methods (tests and specialized tools) and the empirical basis for interpreting their data. This chapter addresses these empirical foundations for *Miller* sentencing and resentencing evaluations.

The scope of the developmental, clinical, and criminological empirical foundations for *Miller* evaluations is broad. It must cover juveniles and young adults in *Miller* sentencing cases as well as adults in *Miller* resentencing cases. Both types of cases may require a developmental and clinical history, so clinical knowledge and inferences may involve developmental periods across the life span. All research on the juvenile justice system is important, but *Miller* examiners must be well informed about the criminal justice system as well, because that is the prospective rehabilitation context for a *Miller* defendant.

This chapter reviews research relevant for a portion of that broad scope. It focuses narrowly on research with special relevance for questions in most *Miller* sentencing and resentencing cases consistent with the legal and developmental constructs reviewed in Chapter 2.

Before proceeding, Table 3.1 (adapted from Woolard & Fountain, 2016) offers some terms used in research to define various types and patterns of offending. Studies sometimes define these terms differently. In addition, studies may use data that are based on different ways of identifying an offense: for example,

Table 3.1 Definitions of Terms Referring to Types/Patterns of Offending

Term	Definition
Offense	Any misdemeanor or felony
Serious offense	Usually felonies (e.g., person, property, drug and weapons offenses)
Violent offense	Involves force or threat of force (e.g., FBI Uniform Crime Reporting system: murder and nonnegligent manslaughter, forcible rape, robbery, aggravated assault, and some sex offenses)
Specialized	Refers to individuals whose offense histories manifest a specific type of offense rather than a variety of types
Prevalence	The number of people within a demographic group (e.g., women or men) who are victimized during a specific time period
Incidence	The number of separate victimizations, or incidents, perpetrated against people within a demographic group during a specific time period
Desistance	Cessation or marked decrease in offending after a developmental period of frequent offending
Persistent	Offending continuously or frequently across some age period
Chronic	Identifies individuals whose offending begins early (e.g., late childhood), increases through adolescence, and continues into adulthood
Context	Classification of an offense incident according to social context or motivation (see Table 3.2)

arrests, convictions, or self-report of illegal behavior. Some studies examine general adolescent samples and others delinquent adolescent samples, and the latter may examine general delinquency or violent offending specifically. In recidivism studies, offenders may be followed for shorter or longer times. Thus, one must pay close attention to variations across apparently similar research studies when comparing them and making inferences using them.

For these reasons, we urge forensic mental health clinicians to consult reviews of relevant studies in the areas in question, rather than relying on single studies, when using research to interpret their assessment results. As noted for topics throughout this chapter, reviews have been written by researchers who have examined the full range of studies and their complexity to arrive at a meaningful consensus of the results and their limitations. Single studies might be outliers in this context. The following discussions often cite such reviews when they are available.

This chapter identifies research relevant for *Miller* evaluations related to (a) correlates of juvenile violent and persistent offending and juvenile homicide, (b) developmental neuroscience and behavioral research on normative adolescents' immaturity, (c) relevant personality and mental health characteristics of young offenders, (d) the efficacy of rehabilitation and treatment methods for young offenders, and (e) available psychological instruments designed to assess young offenders' decisional, dependency, and rehabilitation capacities and potentials.

Ideally, this chapter would include reliable research on how forensic evaluators have been conducting *Miller* evaluations and how courts have been using them. However, no relevant data were available at the time the book was written.

Patterns of Serious Offending by Juveniles

This section reviews fundamental research on (a) correlates of serious and violent offending in youth, (b) life-course trajectories of youthful offenders, and (c) youth homicide.

Serious and Violent Offending and Re-offending

Only a minority of juvenile arrests are for serious or violent offenses (Laub & Sampson, 2003; Piquero et al., 2012). The great majority of arrests are for misdemeanors, property, substance use, and other nonviolent crimes. Most youths arrested for serious or violent offenses are not frequent offenders, but some will more frequently or persistently offend. Less than 10% of juvenile offenders are frequent offenders during adolescence, but they account for more than 50% of recorded juvenile offenses and a disproportionate number of juvenile arrests for serious and violent offenses (Farrington, 1986; Loeber et al., 1998; Wolfgang, Figlio, & Sellin, 1972).

Many variables have been reliably identified as related to risk of repeat offending. (See, generally, DeMatteo et al., 2016; Heilbrun et al., 2005; Hirschi, 2002; also subsequent section in this chapter on "Life-Course Trajectories for Offending"). Among these, for example, are age of first arrest, frequency (chronicity) of offending during adolescence, family dysfunction and early abuse, personality factors (e.g., callous-unemotional traits, antisocial attitudes), behavioral health factors (e.g., substance use), psychosocial factors (e.g., risk taking, impulsivity), and environmental risk factors (e.g., neighborhood, gang/peer influences).

These variables, while related to offending, appear to have limited predictive value for distinguishing future serious or violent offending from future general, less serious offending (Piquero et al., 2003; Sampson & Laub, 2003). This is in part because youth who reoffend tend not to "specialize" in a type of crime, but rather are arrested for a range of nonviolent offenses as well (Gottfredson & Hirschi, 1990; Piquero et al., 2003). While some of the factors noted in the previous paragraph increase risk for future violent offending, many youths who are low on the relevant factors (e.g., low prior offense frequencies, or no prior violent offenses) nevertheless commit violent acts, creating substantial false-positive rates when predicting violent offending (Bersani et al., 2009).

The risk of violent offending by juveniles (persistent or nonpersistent) is influenced also by exposure to violence. Other factors being equal, risk of violence is greater for youths who live in neighborhoods where violence is more frequent, which tend to be communities experiencing serious economic disadvantage and social instability (Sampson, 2012; Sharkey et al., 2017; Weisburd et al., 2004). In addition, there is a remarkable relationship between engaging in violent crime and having been the victim of violence in childhood or during adolescence (Becker & Kerig, 2011; Lauritsen & Laub, 2007).

Age itself is a risk factor for violent behavior (see, generally, Laub & Sampson, 2003). The well-known age–crime curve—rising dramatically across adolescence, peaking in young adulthood, then declining steadily to the late 20s or early 30s—is found for both general crime and for violent crime. This age-pattern has been the focus of much research on desistance from general and violent offending in the late-adolescent and early adult years. Those studies are reviewed in the next discussion.

Life-Course Trajectories for Offending

Trajectory studies seek to identify patterns in the development of aggression, general offending, or serious and violent offending across the life span. They are especially focused on patterns of desistance or persistence in offending, identifying those who are more likely or less likely to be chronic offenders. Of special importance for *Miller* sentencing cases are studies that examine persistence in offending beyond the peak of the age–crime curve in young adulthood.

Trajectory studies are numerous, some examining aggression from infancy through childhood (e.g., Tremblay et al., 2004), for the adolescent years alone (e.g., Piquero et al., 2005), for adolescence into young adulthood (e.g., Monahan et al., 2009), and for adolescence through long-range adulthood (e.g., Lahey et al., 2006; Laub & Sampson, 2003). Russell and Odgers (2016) and Piquero (2008) provide recent, concise reviews.

Generally, these studies affirm Moffitt's (1993) hypothesis (see Chapter 2) regarding the "life-course-persistent" and "adolescent-limited" typology as a useful heuristic, although studies often find several trajectories within Moffitt's two types. Studies broadly support an age-related increase in aggression and offending in late childhood and early adolescence, peaking in the late teens to the mid-20s, and then decreasing markedly. Late-adolescent desistance, therefore, is the norm. Studies find that among youth with persistent, frequent offending in adolescence, only a small proportion—ranging from 1% to 10% in various studies—become chronic non-desistance offenders into their late 20s (Piquero, 2008; Russell & Odgers, 2016).

Desistance of offending in young adulthood does not always mean termination of offending, but rather a marked reduction. Youths with partial desistance as they age into adulthood continue to have burdens of mental and physical health problems and socioeconomic hardship, which in turn places them at a continuing degree of risk of reoffending (Bersani & Doherty, 2018; Russell & Odgers, 2016). However, summarizing past trajectory studies and results from the Pathways to Desistance study, Mulvey (2011) concluded that "most youth who commit felonies greatly reduce their offending over time, regardless of the intervention" (p. 1).

A few studies have examined trajectories and desistance by race and gender. There is some suggestion that desistance among Black males, although following similar trajectories to those we have already noted, may occur somewhat later in age (Loeber et al., 2015; Piquero, 2015). Trajectory studies with females are too few to offer guidance.

One factor for judging likelihood of chronic offending into adulthood has been early age of onset of delinquent activity—that is, in the preteen years (see, generally, Farrington, 2005). Yet the mere fact of early onset is not a strong predictor of persistence into adulthood, because some youth who are abnormally aggressive in the preteen years become less aggressive by the time they reach adolescence (Tremblay, 2004). However, the combination of early onset together with frequent offending during adolescence increases the risk of persistence beyond the adolescent years, although it does not accurately predict it.

The Pathways to Desistance study (Monahan et al., 2009; Mulvey et al., 2010) examined the trajectory-related characteristics of older-adolescent, high-frequency, serious offenders who had recently been involved in the juvenile justice system and were followed into adulthood on release. Persisters tended to have greater deficits in psychosocial maturity (e.g., impulse control, future orientation). When these variables were combined with other variables (e.g., deviant peers, substance use), the studies' five trajectory types were discriminated fairly well, but the psychosocial variables did not effectively predict the main persisting from desisting groups. Likewise, in a review of eighty relevant studies, Jolliffe et al. (2017) found that psychosocial factors did not reliably distinguish young offenders who persist in criminal activity into adulthood. This finding might reflect discontinuity (between-person variability) in development of psychosocial skills from adolescence to adulthood.

Homicide

Research on juvenile homicide is of special relevance for *Miller* sentencing and resentencing cases. According to Federal Bureau of Investigation statistics (2013), about 10% of all major felony arrests in the United States involve youth younger than 18. Within that age group, homicide accounts for less than 1% of felony arrests and about 6% of arrests for serious felonies. Most homicide arrests involve males, although recent literature offers some data on homicide by adolescent and adult women (Heide et al., 2012; Heide & Sellers, 2014).

Homicides involve the death of a victim, but there are several ways to classify homicides for legal and clinical or research purposes, as defined in Table 3.2. Legal classifications codify homicides according to degree of culpability, based on presumptions about the individual's intent at the moment of the homicide, with sentences decreasing in severity for conviction of homicides with lesser intent. Victim classifications also are useful for research purposes and for clinical analyses. About half of victims of youth homicides are acquaintances and about one-third are strangers (Ewing, 1990). Murder of parents is comparatively rare (e.g., less than 10% of juvenile murders: Ewing, 1990), often by children in abusive families (Heide, 1992, 1993; Heide & Petee, 2007).

Table 3.2 also shows some ways in which researchers have classified youth homicides according to motivation, situation, or pathology. They differ in terminology but have some essential

Table 3.2 | Approaches to Homicide Classification

Legal Types	
First-degree murder (both willful and premeditated)	
Felony murder (allows first-degree murder to be charged for killing that occurs during a dangerous felony, even though defendant is not the killer)	
Second-degree murder (intended but not premeditated, or done with disregard for human life	
Voluntary manslaughter (no prior intent, such as a killing that occurs "in the heat of passion" that would cause reasonable person to be emotionally compelled)	
(Source: https://dictionary.findlaw.com/definition/murder.html)	
Motivation-Based Classification Schemes in Social Sciences	
Jenkins & Bell (1993)	Instrumental (during another felony)
	Expressive (during rage or passion)
	Gang-related (while influenced by gang)
Cornell et al. (1987)	Crime-related (during another felony)
	Conflict-related (interpersonal motive)
	Psychotic (related to mental illness)
Cornell et al. (1996)	Instrumental (goal-directed, predatory)
	Reactive (in response to encountered high-stress situations)
Tolan (2007)	Predatory (goal-directed, prior intention)
	Situational (reactive)
	Relationship (in context of personal relation with victim)
	Pathological (in context of a mental illness)

similarities, especially regarding two types. First, all the typologies have a classification for murder during other felonies (e.g., robbery, rape), variously called instrumental, predatory, or crime-related. Second, they have a category for homicides committed in retaliation, in anger, or in the context of stress or threat, labeled expressive, conflict-related, or reactive. Tolan's (2007) typology separates the reactive type into relationship murders (e.g., killing girlfriends/boyfriends or family members) and situational murders (e.g., gang encounters). In urban areas, about half of youth homicides occur in groups or gangs (Loeber et al., 2005).

Some studies using these typologies have found differences in case characteristics related to type of homicide. For example, Cornell et al. (1987) found that instrumental offenders were distinguished from reactive offenders by past violent crime behavior and level of psychopathology. In their Chicago youth homicide sample, Jenkins and Bell (1997) found race differences in types of homicides. About half of White youth homicides were gang-related, compared to one-third of Black youth homicides, while the figures were reversed for expressive homicide. (Such findings, however, are sometimes specific to a study's geographic sample.) Comparing crime-related to conflict-related homicide samples, Benedek and Cornell (1990) found that the crime-related group had significantly greater school-adjustment problems, frequency of prior criminal activity, and substance abuse, while the conflict-related group had a significantly greater likelihood of stress-related events prior to the offense. Khachatryan (2015; Khachatryan et al., 2016) found that crime-related youth homicides were more likely to involve accomplices, but less likely to involve guns, than were conflict-related homicides, but the two did not differ on age of first offense or age of the homicide offense.

Several studies have examined whether youth committing homicide can be distinguished from youth who commit other serious, violent offenses. This search for homicide-specific predictors is difficult for several reasons. The low base rate of a behavior decreases the likelihood of finding reliable predictors without excessive false positives. Moreover, as noted earlier, youth tend not to specialize in specific types of criminal behaviors. Finally, the difference between a murder and an assault conviction sometimes is related to unpredictable circumstances (e.g., quality of the weapon, movement of the target), not to characteristics of the individual.

Baglivio and Wolff (2017), examining a group of offenders in early adolescence and following them prospectively, found that those who committed homicide by age 18 were significantly more likely (at age 13) to have mental illness in their family and have elevated levels of anger/aggression. Most other studies, however, have found few differences. Examining the Pittsburgh Youth Survey cohort, Ahonen et al. (2015) found no differences between adolescent homicide and non-homicide serious offenders in childhood variables (e.g., abuse and neglect), delinquent friends, school performance, or prior violent behaviors. DiCataldo and Everett (2008) largely found the same, except for differences related to the offense itself (e.g., homicide youth more likely to have access to a gun and to evidence substance use at the time of the offense). They noted that where trends in differences were found, the homicide youths tended to show fewer early risk signs than non-homicide serious offenders. Similarly, Benedek and Cornell (1990) found no differences between homicide youth and other adolescent violent offenders in family dysfunction, prior violent offenses, or behavioral health problems. In their sample, however, homicide youth—and especially those with conflict-related homicides—were significantly less likely to have engaged in frequent prior criminal activity and less likely to have school-adjustment problems or early childhood symptoms.

Especially relevant for *Miller* resentencing cases are those studies that have examined recidivism of juvenile homicide offenders while they were on parole after having served adult prison sentences, in most cases after incarceration for eight to 15 years. Based on an average juvenile age at time of homicide (about 15 to 17), time of release on average across studies would appear to have been in the late 20s to early 30s. Most studies collected post-release recidivism data for more than 6 years and as much as 30 years in one study (Khatchatryan, 2015). Study samples have ranged from small (e.g., 25 to 35) to substantial (e.g., over 200).

For these paroled juvenile homicide offender samples, rates of post-release recidivism for any offense have been reported as low as 32% (DiCataldo et al., 2017) and as high as 88% (Khachatryan, 2015; Khachatryan et al., 2016). More typical have been recidivism rates of 50% to 65% (Hagan, 1997; Heide et al., 2001; Trulson et al., 2012; Vries & Liem, 2011), which is comparable to rates of recidivism for prison parolees in general (68% to 77%: Durose, Cooper, & Snyder, 2014). In these studies of youthful homicide offenders released after serving adult sentences, a substantial proportion of post-prison rearrests were for felonies, including robbery or assault, but post-release homicides were very rare.

Generally, studies of youth homicide parolees have found no distinguishing features of those who do and do not recidivate (Hagan, 1997; Khachatryan, 2015; Toupin, 1993). Similarly, Khachatryan (2015) reported no post-release recidivism differences between youths whose homicides had been crime or conflict-related, although youth whose homicides were with associates had higher post-release recidivism rates.

Some studies have examined length of incarceration time in relation to post-release recidivism. Two studies have found that shorter terms were related to greater recidivism (Caudill & Trulson, 2016; Trulson et al., 2012). Many persons in these samples, however, had been serving extended sentences in juvenile facilities, resulting in their release at 21 when they were still at an age for greater recidivism risk. In contrast, DiCataldo et al. (2017) found no relation between post-release recidivism and time served among persons who had served homicide sentences in adult corrections.

Finally, in two studies with youth homicide samples (Caudill & Trulson, 2016; Trulson et al., 2012), incidents of assault on staff or peers and program disruption during incarceration were related to increased rates of recidivism. However, homicide prisoners in general appear not to account for a disproportionate share of prison violence and to be no more likely than other prisoners to be involved in disciplinary misconduct (Reidy et al., 2012; Sorensen & Cunningham, 2008).

Adolescent Development, Decision Making, and Risk Taking

In its decisions in *Roper* through *Montgomery*, the U.S. Supreme Court was influenced in part by research demonstrating adolescents' immaturity in decision making, especially their risk-taking behavior (Levick & Feierman, 2016). This research examined brain developmental during adolescence, as well as behavioral research examining youths' greater risk taking compared to adults. Most of this research emerged in the late 1990s and is continuing. As a body, the research demonstrated the immaturity of adolescents' decisional capacities and their greater risk taking compared to adults, wherein the Court found reason to consider juveniles less culpable for purposes of sentencing for serious offenses. As described in Chapters 1 and 2, the Court also used research to direct future courts to apply this logic on an individual basis.

Forensic examiners, therefore, must be familiar with the evidence from these studies when asked to explain how and why youths' decision making is different from that of adults in ways that bear on courts' decisions about their culpability. The following is a brief review of findings from neuroimaging and behavioral studies of developmental changes with implications for youths' decision making. The research is quite extensive, and the following summary does not cite the many individual studies. Examiners may consult Luna and Wright (2016) for a comprehensive yet accessible summary with citations. Implications for justice policy are examined in Scott and Steinberg (2005), Steinberg (2009, 2013), and Steinberg and Scott (2003).

Neuroimaging studies of brain development have used both cross-sectional (by age) and longitudinal (same individuals as they age) designs, often replicated across methods, labs, and nations. Neuroimaging of brain maturation examines structural changes in gray and white matter, as well as functional changes.

Regarding structural changes, basic areas of the brain are fully formed and have achieved their final weight or volume during the first decade of life. In the second decade, they undergo fine-tuning such as synaptic pruning (removal of neurons to improve networking) and myelination (growth of sheaths on neurons, which improves efficiency of transmission). Much of this fine-tuning is in the region of the prefrontal cortex and its network of neural connections with other areas of the brain. The prefrontal cortex is well known for managing executive functions, such as working memory; regulating emotions and impulses; planning; and monitoring one's own problem-solving process.

Studies of functional brain maturation examine age-related changes in neural reactions within areas of the brain during sensory stimulation. They do this by measuring blood-oxygen level changes in those areas in response to the brain's reaction to external stimuli or during a task requiring processing of information and a response to it (e.g., antisaccade and go/no-go tasks) (Luna & Wright, 2016). Better performance on tasks of this nature requires brain functioning that inhibits (suppresses) impulsive reactions.

Two areas of the brain show significant activation and significant change in performance on those tasks across the second decade of life. One area is the prefrontal lobe, responsible for suppressing impulse and improving goal-directed decisions. These changes continue gradually throughout adolescence until reaching adult levels in the late teens to mid-20s. The other significant change is in the limbic area, especially the amygdala, which is involved in processing emotions. The amygdala manifests a marked increase in responsiveness to reward and threat stimuli. This increase in responsivity begins during hormonal changes in puberty, peaks in mid-adolescence, then subsides in the late teens.

This increase in the amygdala's emotional reactivity, together with the prefrontal lobe's relative immaturity for controlling emotion during decision making, creates a greater risk of poorly modulated decisions and choices in adolescence. (In Chapter 2, see the section on "maturity gap" and "dual systems" concepts.) The result is a potentially greater tendency for risk taking in adolescence, especially in emotion-laden situations. A substantial body of neuroimaging research offers evidence for adolescents' greater tendency, compared to adults, toward risk taking, impulsiveness, and sensation seeking when making choices (e.g., Kahn et al., 2015; Smith et al., 2015; for a review, Steinberg, 2008). In addition, in neuroimaging and behavioral studies, risk taking is increased in adolescents more than in adults when engaged in tasks with recognition that peers are observing their performance (e.g., Chein et al., 2011; Dumontheil et al., 2016; Smith et al., 2015).

A significant body of behavioral studies has found results consistent with the neuroimaging studies and the dual systems concept. One of the major sources of this information is the MacArthur Juvenile Capacity Study (Steinberg et al., 2009), a multi-site national project involving almost 1,000 participants aged 10 to 30. The researchers administered a wide array of psychological tests and self-report questionnaires, as well as laboratory performance tasks, examining risk perception, impulsiveness, sensation seeking, reward sensitivity, preference for immediate or delayed rewards, planning during decision making, consideration of future consequences, and resistance to peer influence. Across adolescence and on multiple measures, results indicated a steady decline in impulsiveness and influence by peers, and a mid-adolescence increase and then decline in sensation seeking and preference for risky options, Adolescents did not perceive themselves as less vulnerable to negative consequences of risky situations than did adults (e.g., Millstein & Halpern-Felsher, 2002; Reyna & Farley, 2006). Instead, in comparison to adults, adolescents tended to weigh the rewards more heavily than the potential negative outcomes, referred to as "reward bias" (Shulman & Cauffman, 2013).

Most *Miller* sentencing defendants will be older adolescents or young adults at the time of evaluation. Much of the research we have cited finds that brain development and age-related behavioral correlates are beginning to approximate adult levels in young adults but are still in transition. Cohen et al. (2016), for example, found that the response of emerging adults (ages 18 to 21) to functional neuroimaging risk-taking tasks were more like adolescents' impulsive responses than those of adults when facing negative (aversive) stimuli but more like adults' responses when facing positive (attractive) stimuli.

Neuroimaging studies identified normative neurobiological development and have been influential in driving law and juvenile justice policy during the past 15 years. However, the state of neuroimaging science does not allow the use of individual brain scans to identify a person's neurobiological degree of maturity (Luna & Wright, 2016; Steinberg, 2009).

Research on Personality and Mental Health Problems

In Chapter 2 we noted that several personality and mental health concepts are relevant when addressing irreparable corruption and the *Miller* developmental factors. This section examines research on personality traits (e.g., psychopathy) and forms of mental health problems relevant for inferences often made in *Miller* evaluations. We use "mental health problems" to refer broadly and collectively to mental health symptoms (with or without psychiatric diagnoses), substance use problems, and trauma-related conditions. This section reviews relevant research on (a) psychopathy and callous-unemotional traits, (b) prevalence of mental health problems and trauma in young offender populations, and (c) mental health problems and adolescent offending.

Psychopathy and Callous-Unemotional Traits

As described in Chapter 2, psychopathy in adults is a chronic and persistent personality disorder. Ample research evidence supports the relation between psychopathy and both general and violent offending in adults (Hart, 1998; Vincent & Hart, 2012). If psychopathy were identifiable during adolescence, this would be of interest in *Miller* sentencing cases in which future prospects for rehabilitation are considered, because psychopathy has been considered relatively resistant to interventions aimed at reducing offending.

Research indicates that one feature of adult psychopathy ("callous-unemotional traits") is very common during adolescent development of adults with psychopathic personality (Frick & White, 2008). However, using callous-unemotional traits measured during adolescence as a predictor of psychopathy in adulthood has limited value (for reviews, see DeMatteo et al., 2010; Vincent et al., 2016). This is because many youths who manifest high callous-unemotional traits do not develop psychopathy in adulthood, producing high false-positive rates when these traits are used as a predictor (e.g., Cauffman et al., 2016; Lynam et al., 2007). A recent comprehensive review of relevant studies concluded that they "have not established a sufficiently high level of stability . . . to warrant testimony about whether a youth has psychopathic personality disorder" (Vincent et al., 2016, p. 219).

The reasons for these findings are likely due to the developmental context of adolescence, which includes discontinuities, continued differentiation (personality traits still forming), and normative risk taking during adolescence. For similar reasons, Conduct Disorder (CD) during adolescence is characteristic of adults with Antisocial Personality Disorder, but only about one-third of youth diagnosed with CD during adolescence meet criteria for Antisocial Personality Disorder in adulthood (e.g., Odgers et al., 2008). In addition, some relatively normal but often transient behavioral and emotional characteristics of adolescence (e.g., self-centered, fail to consider others) are similar to callous-unemotional traits and may contribute to false-positive errors when predicting later psychopathy (Edens et al., 2001; Seagrave & Grisso, 2002).

Prevalence of Mental Health Problems in Adolescent Offenders

Studies have consistently found that between 50% and 70% of youth in juvenile justice settings (e.g., pretrial detention) meet criteria for one or more behavioral health disorders, a proportion substantially greater than in the general youth population (e.g., Shufelt & Cocozza, 2006; Teplin et al., 2002; Wasserman et al., 2002). Across studies, the most common disorders are CD, substance use disorders, depressive and anxiety disorders, trauma- and stressor-related disorders, and Attention-Deficit/Hyperactivity Disorder (ADHD; Grisso, 2004).

Especially prevalent in delinquent populations is prior exposure to potentially traumatizing experiences, often multiple, found in almost all youth in delinquency samples (e.g., 90%: Abram et al., 2004). Mere exposure to traumatic events does not imply lasting effects or diagnostic conditions. But justice-involved youth are more likely than youth in general to be exposed to multiple violent and potentially traumatizing experiences (Abram et al., 2013). Moreover, Post-Traumatic Stress Disorder (PTSD) is found much more frequently in delinquent samples than in the general youth population (Abram et al., 2013; Becker & Kerig, 2011; Dierkhising et al., 2013). Trauma's potential impact is not confined to PTSD, however, as traumatic stress symptoms represent a continuum in terms of severity and type (Zelechoski, 2016), and the effects of traumatic stress may have consequences that manifest as symptoms of other disorders (e.g., depression or anxiety disorders).

Most youth with any disorder at the time of assessment manifest comorbid conditions (e.g., Abram et al., 2013; Teplin et al., 2002), often transient rather than persistent across time (Mash & Barkley, 2014). This suggests the need for present diagnosis to be considered together with mental health records regarding the course of mental health problems across the individual's adolescent years (Grisso, 2004). In addition, some disorders arise only in early adulthood and are difficult to anticipate from assessment during adolescence (American Psychiatric Association, 2013).

Mental Health Problems and Offending During Adolescence

Analyses of *Miller*'s offense context factor will sometimes raise the question of the relation of a youth's mental disorder to the offense. There is ample evidence that some disorders increase the likelihood of immature risk taking and offending beyond the norm for adolescents (e.g., Davis & Vander Stoep, 1997; Ford et al., 2006, 2012; Kazdin, 2000; Maschi et al., 2008; Mash & Barkley, 2014; Nagel et al., 2016; Zelechoski, 2016).

How this is to be construed, however, is complex. As reviewed earlier, factors like impulsiveness, anger, and immature risk taking are related to youth offending. These conditions can be manifested in youths with no serious mental disorders. These same conditions, however, are symptoms of some disorders in adolescence—for example, impulsiveness associated with ADHD, anger related to adolescent depression, and PTSD symptoms of irritability, recklessness, and hypervigilant reactivity. Yet, many forms of mental health problems do not include impulsiveness, anger, or risk-taking tendencies. Thus, Schubert et al. (2011) found that simply having a mental disorder was not significantly related to youth offending. This suggests that it is not "mental disorder" itself that contributes to offending, but whether the form of mental disorder includes symptoms that contribute to specific conditions that increase generally the risk of offending. Mental health problems, therefore, will sometimes be important to consider in analyses of the offense context in *Miller* cases.

In addition, it is important to consider the potential impact of chronic and persistent mental disorder during childhood and adolescence on a youth's development. When persistent throughout childhood and adolescence, mental health problems can influence the development of the brain, given its plasticity during the cognitive and psychosocial maturation process (e.g., for effects of childhood traumatic stress, see Nemeroff, 2004). Clinically significant episodes of psychopathology can also produce delays in normal cognitive and psychosocial development, extending a youth's immaturity beyond age expectancies (Mash & Barkley, 2014).

Research on Rehabilitation and Treatment of Young Offenders

Previous chapters established that *Miller* sentencing and resentencing cases will examine prospects for rehabilitation. In Chapter 2 we offered an interactive approach to the question of rehabilitation potential, including (a) characteristics of the individual (which we called "amenability") and (b) a consideration of available interventions and their quality (which we called "appropriate interventions"). Ultimately, inferences about prospects for rehabilitation also must consider the likelihood that the intervention provided will match the individual's needs and characteristics. The scope of relevant research, therefore, would focus on variables related to individuals' amenability, the qualities and degrees of effectiveness of various possible interventions, and the interaction between them.

Any consideration of prospects must look back at past rehabilitation efforts, as well as forward to possible future interventions. Research to inform the look at past interventions must be based on the age of the defendant at the time of the intervention as well as the nature of the interventions themselves. When the analysis turns to future prospects, research on the amenability of adolescents in juvenile settings is less relevant than research on young adults, because most *Miller* sentencing examinees will be 18 to 20 at the time of their sentencing evaluations and will be offered correctional program rehabilitation during their 20s and 30s. For *Miller* resentencing cases, research on amenability of young- to middle-aged adults, including their prospects for parole services, will be relevant—as will responses to interventions that have been provided.

Despite the potentially broad scope of research relevant for questions of prospects for rehabilitation, research on amenability (for any ages) has not been substantial. Somewhat more is known about the quality of juvenile justice and adult correctional interventions.

Characteristics of the Individual (Amenability)

A review earlier in this chapter ("Adolescent Development, Decision Making, and Risk Taking") examined neuroimaging and behavioral research with adolescents. Those studies indicate that brain and behavioral development are ongoing into the early to mid-20s, offering opportunities for rehabilitation and therapeutic interventions to influence development before maturation is completed. That research supports the view that, generally, amenability is a normative characteristic of youth because of their developmentally immature status, although there is individual variability in this characteristic at any age.

Research on two types of characteristics of the individual are relevant for amenability to rehabilitation: (a) individual characteristics that need to change and (b) individual characteristics that promote or challenge change. The Risk-Needs-Responsivity (RNR) model described in Chapter 2 conceptualizes these two components and has generated a substantial research base when applied in juvenile and adult offender rehabilitation (Andrews et al., 1990; DeMatteo et al., 2016; Hoge, 2016). RNR focuses on identification of criminogenic factors (e.g., educational, occupational, familial or peer relations) as targets for intervention. It also identifies the importance of identifying individual characteristics that may inhibit or promote the individual's responsiveness to interventions (RNR's specific responsivity component). RNR research has demonstrated better outcomes (reduced recidivism) when criminogenic needs are matched with appropriate interventions, supplemented with adequate attention to responsivity characteristics (Andrews & Dowden, 2005; Koehler et al., 2013).

Salekin's (2015) model of amenability offers a way to think about responsivity factors and to examine research evidence for them. His model identifies three types of factors: (a) type and degree of mental health problems; (b) personality factors suggesting responsibility and motivation to change (e.g., open to influence, experiences sufficient discomfort to motivate participation in rehabilitation efforts); and (c) personality factors suggesting consideration and tolerance of others (e.g., capacity for empathy, social responsiveness).

Regarding the first of these, many mental health conditions (e.g., ADHD, PTSD, mood disorders, chronic stress) and cognitive deficits (e.g., intellectual disability) are relevant for making inferences about responsivity. Their potential for change will depend on the individual's specific disorder and its treatability given known psychopharmacological and psychological methods, as well as its degree of severity and chronicity. For these matters, one must consult clinical research literature specific to the conditions relevant for the individual in question, which will offer reasonable guidance for the treatment amenability of most disorders and deficits.

Regarding Salekin's second and third components, Heilbrun et al. (2017) note that there has been little research with adolescents or young adults demonstrating the relation between various personality variables and treatment outcomes. Page and Scalora (2004) have suggested that a youth's locus of control (beliefs that things happen because of one's own effort versus merely by fate or chance; Rotter, 1966) might offer potential for identifying a youth's degree of amenability. Their review of research suggested that internal locus of control is positively related to outcomes in various clinical settings, although not specifically for juvenile offenders. Indeed, little is known empirically about the relevance of any of the other specific personality variables noted by Salekin (2015) or Grisso (2013) regarding amenability—for example, susceptible to influence, experiences discomfort, empathy, or capacity for social attachments.

Many of those variables, however, have been studied indirectly, because deficits in some of those traits are characteristics of psychopathy and callous-emotional traits, about which there has been relevant research on their implications for treatment. Substantial research has supported the expectation that adults' scores on psychopathy measures or measures of callous-unemotional traits in young people are related to less satisfactory outcomes across various types of interventions with offenders (for reviews: Hawes et al., 2014; Skeem et al., 2002). However, recent treatment-outcome studies have shown that the presence of high scores on those traits does not preclude positive outcomes (e.g., Haneveld et al., 2018; Skeem et al., 2002). Among youth with callous-unemotional traits, research has identified gains in prosocial behaviors with certain interventions (e.g., Caldwell et al., 2006; Salekin et al., 2012; see also Hawes et al., 2014, for a recent review). Reviewing the evidence, Vincent et al. (2016) concluded that "There is no evidence that youths with psychopathic features are incapable of benefitting from treatment or that treatment is contraindicated" (p. 220).

Research on Interventions

Miller sentencing defendants will not be receiving juvenile justice interventions in the future. But the nature and quality of those interventions to which they have been exposed in their past juvenile justice contact will be relevant when assessing their responsiveness to interventions. Examiners are referred to major reviews of an extensive body of research on the efficacy and effectiveness of juvenile justice rehabilitation and treatment interventions (Lipsey, 2009; Lipsey et al., 2001; Viljoen et al., 2016).

According to this body of research, there are a number of juvenile justice interventions that are consistently effective in reducing recidivism and increasing youths' positive development. Most of them are structured, manualized programs based on developmental concepts. Examples include multisystemic therapy (MST; Henggeler et al., 2009), functional family therapy (Alexander et al., 1998), and both cognitive-behavioral therapy and dialectical behavioral therapy. The research describes many other interventions with questionable or negative outcomes, including routine probation, unspecified individual counseling, and programs such as Scared Straight and juvenile bootcamp. Familiarity with the research-based evidence for such programs is important when reviewing a *Miller* defendant's failure to respond to past treatment interventions, because any inferences based on such failure should take into consideration the possibility that the youth was merely exposed to interventions with little value.

Looking ahead to future interventions will be guided in part by research on interventions found in adult secure correctional facilities where defendants will be placed. No body of research examines correctional "best practices" in rehabilitation specifically for homicide offenders (juvenile or adult) in secure adult corrections. The review of juvenile homicide earlier in this chapter, however, provides little evidence that the criminogenic needs associated with recidivism are different for juvenile homicide offenders in general than for other juvenile violent offenders.

In Chapter 2 we described three types of correctional programming relevant for effective rehabilitation. The first is education and employability interventions, and most studies in a very large body of research indicate that those interventions can produce small to moderate reductions in recidivism if they are implemented with integrity (for a recent review: Duwe, 2017). The second category is cognitive restructuring and social skills training. Among these, cognitive-behavioral therapy has been the most studied and identified in meta-analytic reviews as having potential to produce significant reduction in post-release recidivism (e.g., Allen et al., 2001; Lipsey et al., 2007; Wilson et al., 2005).

MST has been among the leading and most successful approaches for juvenile offenders, suggesting the need to develop MST applications for young adults with serious mental illness (Skeem et al., 2011). Modification of MST for this special young adult offender population is in development (Sheidow et al., 2016). A meta-analysis examining substance use treatment programs found that those that used cognitive restructuring methods with fidelity reduced post-release drug use and recidivism (Mitchell et al., 2007).

Finally, virtually all prisons provide mental health services. As reviewed by Skeem et al. (2011), mental health interventions in prison have proven successful in improving clinical outcomes, yet they have produced only weak effects, at best, in reducing recidivism. This may be due in part to deficits in mental health treatment in the community after release. Duwe (2017) suggests, in addition, that too often mental health treatment in prisons presumes that treatment of symptoms themselves is the appropriate objective, so that services related to more critical criminogenic needs may be neglected.

Research on the Relevance of Past Rehabilitation Efforts

In both *Miller* sentencing and resentencing cases, a youth's or adult's past failure to respond may be taken by courts as evidence of lack of amenability. As noted earlier, outcomes represent an interaction between the youth's amenability and the rehabilitation intervention that is applied. Therefore, both the nature and quality of past interventions are relevant when considering possible reasons for an individual's past lack of response. In such analyses, four types of research are relevant.

First, as noted in the previous discussion, youth and adult offenders often are exposed to interventions for which there is no evidence for their value. Moreover, even rehabilitation interventions with evidence-based value have been shown to be effective in practice only if they are implemented according to their manualized procedures (Lipsey, 2009). The fact that a youth has not responded to past interventions may be due to the poor quality of those interventions, not necessarily to the youth's degree of amenability. The same may be true in *Miller* resentencing cases for past interventions the individual was provided in prison.

Second, research with the RNR approach has identified the importance of matching an individual's criminogenic characteristics with evidence-based services specifically designed to address those characteristics (Hoge, 2016; Vieira et al., 2009). Many juvenile and adult correctional systems do not employ an RNR approach or, if they do, they fail to implement the matching procedures that RNR specifies. Cases of poor past outcomes, therefore, may be due to poor matching, not necessarily poor amenability.

Third, the conditions of juvenile and adult corrections facilities in which rehabilitation interventions are employed often are not conducive to promoting the social and emotional health of inmates and may exacerbate it. Their mental health services often must operate in a context of crowding, inadequate resources, and security demands that result in inferior service (Gonzales & Connell, 2014). Moreover, research has shown that when the conditions of juvenile and adult corrections facilities are stressful, abusive, or traumatizing, this can produce the very emotional and social disabilities that rehabilitation seeks to remediate (Dierkhising et al., 2014; Haney, 2003; Lambie & Randell, 2013).

Miller resentencing cases raise the question of prison misconduct during incarceration as potential evidence that the individual was resistant to rehabilitation or that rehabilitation efforts failed. This can be especially relevant for resentencing of individuals who began their prison term during their later adolescence. Kaunliang et al. (2008) found that this group of older juveniles in adult prisons was more likely to engage in prison misconduct than prison inmates in general, especially during their first few years. It is not known whether this is because they are a select group (having committed very serious crimes; see Bechtold & Cauffman, 2015), because they are threatened as younger inmates in an adult prison, or whether their misconduct itself is a transient consequence of their lesser developmental maturity.

Standardized Assessment Instruments

As reviewed in Chapter 5, *Miller* sentencing and resentencing cases will require collection of data from a wide range of sources: records of past offending; documents describing the individual's earlier health and social history (e.g., health, mental health, education); and interviews with the defendant, caretakers, and service providers. As with any forensic evaluation, data collection should be supplemented whenever possible by standardized tests and tools that have demonstrated validity and reliable norms (allowing for age-related developmental comparisons) to assess relevant characteristics of the defendant.

Four basic rules for test selection will apply. First, the test must measure a characteristic that is conceptually relevant regarding the analyses associated with *Miller* cases: that is, relevant as data to address irreparable corruption or the *Miller* factors. Second, the test must be normed and validated for the defendant's current age. Some defendants in *Miller* sentencing cases are no longer adolescents when tested, so adult-normed tests (18 and older) sometimes will be more appropriate. Third, the test must have known validity for use with the demographic characteristics of the defendant, especially gender and race, ethnicity, and/or culture. Finally, consider whether the test has norms for offender samples. For example, prison samples may be especially helpful when conducting *Miller* resentencing cases.

This section describes assessment tools potentially relevant for *Miller* cases, offering references that review them more completely, as well as commentary on their relevance and suitability. They are reviewed in clusters as tools for assessing (a) cognition, risk taking, and decision making, (b) victimization (trauma) and psychosocial characteristics, (c) recidivism risk and rehabilitation potential, and (d) mental health problems.

Cognition, Risk Taking, and Immature Decision Making

Of special relevance in *Miller* cases are an individual's cognitive abilities, cognitive strategies, and cognitive control (impulsiveness) as data for making developmental inferences about the individual's decisional capacities. Several types of psychological instruments offer potential for standardized assessment of these characteristics.

Most basic are intelligence tests (e.g., Wechsler Intelligence Scale for Children-Fifth Edition [WISC-V], 2014; Wechsler Adult Intelligence Scale-Fourth Edition [WAIS-IV], 2008). In addition to providing information on general intelligence, the subtests on these instruments assess performance on tasks requiring ability to form abstractions, ability to process information rapidly but with care, general fund of information, and working memory—all of which have implications for the decisional developmental component in *Miller* analyses. Intelligence test norms provide opportunities for comparison to age peers as well as other age groups. In some cases, examiners may also wish to consider tests used to assess specific learning disabilities with implications for cognitive processing and impulsiveness (Sattler, 2002, 2008). The field offers guidance to clinicians for interpreting tests of intelligence and learning disabilities with racial/ethnic minority adolescents (e.g., Valencia & Suzuki, 2000).

Several neuropsychological and psychological tools have been used in research (neuroimaging and behavioral) to study impulsive and immature responding in tasks that involve risk taking (potentially relevant for the decisional factor). Unfortunately, many of these tools currently have limited utility for forensic examiners (Salekin et al., 2016). First, some are difficult to obtain because they have not been made available commercially. Second, for most of them there are insufficient data on their use in forensic contexts where chances of lack of effort or feigning are increased, or with forensic populations with racial and cultural proportions that might not be represented in research data on the tools. Third, some of the tools do not have age-graded norms appropriate for comparative use. Fourth, how the tools might withstand Daubert or Frye tests is unknown.

With these cautions, the tools are mentioned in the following discussion primarily for their potential development of further research on their forensic use. Moreover, in their testimony, *Miller* examiners may be asked about these tools, or may want to describe them, in the context of explaining research supporting our knowledge of adolescents' decision-making capacities.

The Go/No-Go Association Task (Nosek & Banaji, 2001) and the Stroop Color and Word Test (Golden, 1978) are timed tasks (rewarding rapid responding as well as accuracy) that require information processing based on instructions to respond only to certain features when they appear visually in test stimuli. Good performance requires efficient suppression of impulsive responses to potential miscues. Other standardized tasks relevant for assessing behavioral-emotional control during decision making are measures of reward sensitivity (e.g., Iowa Gambling Task: Bechara et al., 1994) and preferences for immediate versus delayed rewards (e.g., Delay Discounting Task: Green et al., 1999). The Tower of London Task (Berg & Byrd, 2002; Culbertson & Zillmer, 2005) rewards efficient planning before committing to options.

Risk-taking preferences and attitudes have been assessed by researchers with a variety of structured self-report questionnaires or interview schedules. Among them are measures of a youth's consideration of short- versus long-range consequences (Consideration of Future Consequences Scale: Strathman et al., 1994; Future Outlook Inventory: Cauffman & Woolard, 1999; Future Orientation: Steinberg et al., 2007), perceived risk and risk preference (Benthin Risk Perception Measure: Benthin et al., 1993; Zuckerman Sensation-Seeking Scale: Zuckerman et al., 1978), impulsiveness (Barratt Impulsiveness Scale: Patton et al., 1995), and degree of peer influence during decision making (Resistance to Peer Influence: Steinberg & Monahan, 2007).

As noted earlier, many of these tools currently have limited utility for forensic evaluations in *Miller* cases. A later section of this chapter ("Risk Assessment") reviews a standardized tool, designed specifically for forensic cases, that assesses certain immature risk-taking characteristics as well as recidivism.

Victimization and Psychosocial Dependency

Miller's dependency factor emphasizes consideration of the youth's victimization (e.g., family dysfunction, poverty, traumatizing experiences) as well as the youth's own lesser degree of autonomy to deal with their effects. Much of the data for inferences about these matters will derive from historical review of the youth's family, economic, and social environment. Some assessment tools, however, are relevant.

Among them are ways to assess traumatization. Trauma screening and assessment tools typically are paper-and-pencil inventories or structured and scorable interview schedules. There are many types of trauma-related tools for varied purposes, so examiners must choose them based on the specific trauma question to be addressed in a case. Wevodau (2016) has provided comprehensive reviews of each of 11 major trauma-related tools of three types. Strand et al. (2004) offer more concise reviews of 25 trauma-related instruments. They classify them as four types.

First, some trauma-focused tools assess history of exposure to potentially traumatizing experiences, but without assessment of trauma symptoms (e.g., Juvenile Victimization Questionnaire: Finkelhor et al., 2005; Traumatic Events Screening Inventory: Edwards & Rogers, 1997). Second, some assess trauma history and current symptoms diagnostic of PTSD specifically (e.g., Clinician-Administered PTSD Scale for DSM-5—Child/Adolescent Version (CAPS-5): Weathers et al., 2013; Clinician-Administered PTSD Scale for DSM-5—Child/Adolescent Version (CAPS-CA-5): Pynoos et al., 2015; University of California Los Angeles Post Traumatic Stress Disorder Reaction Index: Steinberg et al., 2004). The third and fourth types both assess symptoms of traumatizing experiences. However, one set of tools assesses those symptoms focusing on characteristics of trauma disorders other than PTSD, such as dissociative disorder (e.g., Adolescent Dissociative Experiences Scale: Armstrong et al., 1997). The other type examines history and multiple symptoms of trauma such as depression, anger, and anxiety without focusing on a specific trauma disorder (e.g., Trauma Symptom Checklist for Children: Briere, 1996). Many of these tools have been used in both clinical and research contexts with delinquent youth, and most have application with young adults as well.

The concept of a youth's degree of autonomy versus dependence on others does not have an independent measurement history.

Concepts that might be relevant are capacity for independent judgment versus influence by others, self-confidence, social skills, stability of self-identity, and personal values. Some relevant information regarding these characteristics might be provided by certain scales in general clinical and personality measures often used with adolescents and young adults, as discussed in a later section ("Psychopathy and Mental Health Problems"). In addition, the Vineland-II Adaptive Behavior Scales (Sparrow et al., 2005), appropriate for adolescents through adulthood, assesses daily living skills, communication, and socialization. (See also the Risk-Sophistication-Treatment Inventory reviewed in the next section.)

Risk Assessment

In Chapter 2 we defined "risk assessment" as including three components related to risk: (a) identifying criminogenic factors contributing to past offending; (b) identifying factors that may influence rehabilitation potential to reduce offending; and (c) an estimate of the likelihood of future re-offending (that is, risk of recidivism). We explained that *Miller* resentencing cases often will benefit from all three of these components, while *Miller* sentencing cases will benefit from the first two components but not the third (that is, risk of recidivism scores). Here we describe some common adult and juvenile risk assessment tools that provide for all three components. *Miller* sentencing cases will not find a use for the third component but may benefit from the tools' structure in identifying the first and second components.

The two most common risk assessment tools for adults providing more than a risk-of-recidivism score alone are the Level of Services/Case Management Inventory (LS/CMI: Andrews et al., 2004) and the Historical-Clinical-Risk Management-20: Third Version (HCR-20:3V, Douglas et al., 2013). The LS/CMI uses an actuarial, RNR approach assessing (a) risk of future offending, (b) criminogenic factors contributing to risk (and therefore targeted for rehabilitation to reduce future risk), and (c) responsivity characteristics of the individual. Records and semi-structured interviewing are used to collect data for ratings of 43 items on eight subscales (corresponding to the tool's eight risk domains). This leads to a numerical classification as defined by norms for adults (18 and older). For a review of extensive research on the validity of the LS/CMI, see Andrews et al. (2010).

In contrast, the HCR-20:3V structures a clinician's interview with items related to risk factors in three broad categories: historical, individual, and social/contextual factors. The tool uses a "structured professional judgment" approach to arrive at risk of recidivism, criminogenic factors for past offending, and responsivity decisions based on the clinician's own judgment about the relative weight of the factors in the case in question. For a comprehensive research review of the HRC-20:3V, see Douglas and Shaffer-McCuish (in press).

For juveniles, there are three commonly used risk assessment tools providing more than risk-of-recidivism scores alone. Two of them are youth versions of the two adult risk-assessment tools just described. The Youth Level of Services/Case Management Inventory (YLS/CMI: Hoge & Andrews, 2010) employs the LS/CMI format, but its content has been modified to be developmentally age-relevant and its actuarial components have been empirically derived from research with samples aged 12 through 17. Reviews of extensive research evidence for its validity and limits are provided by Hoge (2016) and DeMatteo et al. (2016). The Structured Assessment of Violence Risk in Youth (SAVRY: Borum et al., 2006). The SAVRY was patterned after the HCR-20's format and structured professional judgment process, but it is built around 24 youth-specific factors, in addition to six protective factors that can inform rehabilitation and risk reduction. See Borum et al. (in press) for a comprehensive review of evidence for the SAVRY's validity.

The third juvenile tool, the Risk-Sophistication-Treatment Inventory (RSTI: Salekin, 2004), was developed specifically to address the risk, sophistication-maturity, and treatment (rehabilitation) amenability questions at the heart of juvenile transfer and disposition cases. For reasons noted earlier, the "risk" component in the RSTI will not be of use for youth in *Miller* sentencing cases. The other two sections of the RSTI, however, assess concepts related to treatment amenability and psychosocial attributes. For example, the RSTI's Sophistication-Maturity scale includes 15 items clustered in three subscales: Autonomy, Cognitive Skills, and Emotional Skills. Norms are provided for ages nine through 18. The tool uses a semi-structured interview together with collateral information related to each of the scales. Research generally has supported the construct validity of the scales (correlating logically with similar concepts and measures), as well as its correspondence to transfer/non-transfer decisions. Examiners can find helpful reviews of the RSTI by Salekin (2016) and Heilbrun et al. (2017).

Psychopathy and Mental Health Problems

As discussed earlier, psychopathy instruments for adults assess personality traits that have relevance for judging rehabilitation potential. The Psychopathy Checklist-Revised (PCL-R: Hare, 2002), designed for persons 18 and older, is the most widely used psychopathy assessment tool. (For a review, see DeMatteo et al., 2010.) Similar measures with juveniles have no established value for predicting psychopathy as youth mature into the adult years (see this chapter's earlier discussion of "Psychopathy and Callous-Unemotional Traits"). In some cases, however, current callous-unemotional traits might be relevant when examining the nature of a youth's past offending (e.g., in offense context analyses). If used for that purpose, several tools focusing on adolescent callous-unemotional traits are available (e.g., Self-Report Antisocial Process Screening, Frick & Hare, 2001; Youth Psychopathic Traits Inventory, Andershed et al., 2002; Inventory of Callous-Unemotional Traits, Frick, 2004), as well as the Psychopathy Checklist: Youth Version (PCL: YV: Forth et al., 2003). These tools are reviewed by Vincent et al. (2016).

Mental health problems (mental or behavioral disorders, substance use, and trauma-related conditions) are relevant for clinical inferences related to all of the *Miller* factors, for reasons described earlier in this chapter and in Chapter 2. Clinicians will be familiar with validated tools commonly used for clinical diagnostic purposes for both adolescents and adults, so a listing of them is not necessary. Measures validated for adults (18 and older) will most often be used in *Miller* cases, given the typical age of *Miller* defendants at the time of evaluation. Clinicians should note that diagnostic instruments providing validated norms with offender or correctional samples may be especially helpful. Examples include the Minnesota Multiphasic Personality Inventory-2-Restructured Form (Ben-Porath & Tellegen, 2008) and the Personality Assessment Inventory (Morey, 1991).

Trauma-related tools were reviewed earlier in this section ("Victimization and Psychosocial Dependency"). Substance use is a key factor in youths' and adults' offending and is relevant for rehabilitation planning. Frequently used and validated tools for assessing substance use include the Substance Abuse Subtle Screening Inventory-Fourth Edition (SASSI-IV; Miller, 2016; this tool has adolescent and adult versions) and, for adults, the Drug Abuse Screening Test (DAST; Skinner, 1982; for a review, Yudko et al., 2007). These instruments also provide comparisons to forensic samples. Finally, ADHD is of frequent concern among young offenders regarding impulsivity and distraction. ADHD assessment often benefits from specialized tools: for example, the Behavior Assessment System for Children (BASC: Reynolds & Kamphaus, 2015).

Conclusion

This chapter has identified research offering an empirical foundation for evaluating characteristics of youth and adults relevant for *Miller* sentencing and resentencing evaluations. Of note, little research was available specifically on *Miller* cases and evaluations when this review was assembled. Therefore, we used the U.S. Supreme Court's factors in *Miller* and *Montgomery* as a guide for selecting and organizing existing empirical evidence—developmental, clinical, criminological, and forensic—suitable for addressing the factors.

The review focused especially on an empirical foundation to guide inferences about violent offending in youth, normative adolescent development and risk taking, relevant personality and mental health factors, research on rehabilitation methods, and evidence-based tools relevant for assessing those areas.

Chapters 1, 2, and 3 have offered the legal, conceptual, and empirical foundations for *Miller* evaluations. The remaining chapters now turn to the structure and process for performing *Miller* sentencing and resentencing evaluations guided by those foundations.

4 Preparation for the Evaluation

Preparing to accept *Miller* or *Montgomery* referrals is a multi-stage process. The first step is particularly important: determining if you have the necessary knowledge, training, and expertise needed to conduct these types of evaluations. Referrals should only be accepted after you have identified and addressed any deficits and are confident in your competence to take on *Miller* cases. Forensic mental health professionals should have familiarity with the appropriate statutes and case law (federal and state), relevant research, an awareness of possible ethical conflicts that may arise in the course of conducting these assessments, and the methodology appropriate to performing the evaluation. The next stage involves extensive communication with a retaining party regarding a specific case, including logistical information. If a clinician decides to accept a referral, the next step involves drafting a timeline and plan for the evaluation. This chapter provides guidance on the types of questions and reflection needed during this process.

Competence: Adequate Knowledge, Training and Expertise

The U.S. Supreme Court equated a sentence of life without parole (LWOP) to the death penalty for those who committed the crime before their eighteenth birthday. This means that *Miller* evaluations require as much specialized expertise as capital sentencing evaluations—if not more. Before taking on a *Miller* case, clinicians should undergo rigorous self-reflection about their current skills, knowledge, logistical capacity, and emotional fortitude.

Scrutinizing one's own possible biases is another critical part of this decision-making process. This is not meant to discourage anyone from pursuing this work, but rather to encourage clinicians to seek the additional training and experience that will make them better equipped.

We anticipate that most *Miller* evaluations will be conducted by a psychologist or a psychiatrist. A good place to begin is the discipline's relevant specialty guidelines. For psychology that is the Specialty Guidelines for Forensic Psychology (American Psychological Association [APA], 2013); for psychiatry, it is the Ethical Guidelines for the Practice of Forensic Psychiatry (American Academy of Psychiatry and the Law, 2005). (For a discussion of issues related to the question of competence and a range of other ethical considerations see Heilbrun et al., 2009; Otto et al., 2017.) Determining competence for *Miller* evaluations is more nuanced than simply asking "How long have I been a practicing clinician?" or "How long have I been conducting forensic evaluations?" It also involves rigorous self-assessment related to both the legal and clinical domains.

Competence in the Legal Domain

From a legal perspective, clinicians should be knowledgeable regarding the law pertaining to the evaluation. They should ask themselves a series of questions about this.

Do I understand the legal issue at hand? This entails reading and understanding the *Miller* and *Montgomery* cases themselves as well as relevant jurisdictional statutes. The clinician's role is to provide the trier of fact with information to consider when determining how to sentence the defendant.

Do I understand how the criminal justice system operates? From a practical and theoretical standpoint, criminal courts function differently than other branches of the legal system (Melton et al., 2018). The adult criminal justice system is more adversarial than the juvenile justice system or the court that handles abuse and neglect cases. Even clinicians with years of experience conducting evaluations for juvenile court or abuse and neglect or divorce proceedings should not assume they are familiar with how the criminal court functions, nor should they assume they are competent to conduct an evaluation to be used in a criminal court matter.

Do I understand how the federal and state rules of evidence apply to my work? Minimally, familiarity with Federal Rules of Evidence (2019) sections 702–705 and the state equivalent in one's jurisdiction is recommended. These rules relate to the methods clinicians use to develop opinions, as well as the types and limits of opinions that can be offered in court. It is important to know both the federal and state rules of evidence because the differences between the two could impact the manner in which one practices. For example, in 2016, the rules governing admissibility of hearsay evidence changed in California (California Evidence Code 804, *People v. Sanchez* (2016). This altered the landscape for expert witnesses relying on hearsay when offering an opinion in criminal court (see Hamilton, 2018, for a discussion of this issue).

Am I familiar with the debate around ultimate legal issues testimony? Federal Rules of Evidence 704 is particularly important because it specifies that, with two exceptions, a clinician can testify to the ultimate legal issues. However, for many years forensic mental health scholars have debated the appropriateness of an expert providing ultimate issue testimony. Some argue this testimony is beyond the purview of a clinician's expertise (Heilbrun, 2001; Melton et al., 2018; Tillbrook et al., 2003). Others (Rogers & Ewing, 2003) argue this is something a clinician should provide, or have empirically demonstrated (Redding et al., 2001) that it is something judges and lawyers expect of an expert witness. Arnold et al. (2018) have specifically considered the ultimate issue as it applies to *Miller* evaluations and argued that clinicians should avoid answering the ultimate legal question directly. We strongly encourage clinicians to understand both sides of this argument and decide where they stand, while being cognizant of the fact that, with some clearly defined exceptions, testifying as to the ultimate issue is not legally prohibited.

Do I understand how prisons and jails function? Due to the nature of the crime, the defendant may have spent a lengthy period in jail or prison prior to being evaluated. Consequently, the clinician should understand how these institutions function, at least with respect to disciplinary policies and write-ups, programs and services available to detainees/inmates, opportunities for detainees/inmates to work in the facility, and the ways in which long-term incarceration may influence behavior.

Clinicians are also encouraged to contemplate their own comfort levels within these settings, as this could affect competence. A clinician might understand how the system operates but be uncomfortable working within it because of its penal nature. Most of these defendants will be detained at the time of the evaluation. Clinicians substantially ill at ease in high-security correctional environments should not accept referrals that involve detained defendants. By examining both one's understanding and comfort levels, the clinician can identify areas where additional training and experience might be needed.

Competence in the Clinical-Forensic Domain

The demand for *Miller* (re)sentencing or *de facto* life sentencing evaluations is fairly recent. Experience with other kinds of forensic evaluations does not necessarily translate into competence with those related to *Miller*. For example, one study (Rodway et al., 2011) examined forensic reports submitted about juvenile homicide offenders. Reports written by child and adolescent–trained clinicians provided more developmental information than those authored by clinicians without such training. Some important questions related to *Miller* competence in the clinical domain are discussed in this section.

Do I understand the issue of response style as it applies to evaluating juveniles as well as adults—and how to assess response style as part of an evaluation? This issue is not unique to *Miller* evaluations. However, depending on the populations and settings with which a clinician is most familiar, additional knowledge relevant to other age groups might be needed (DeRight & Carone, 2015; McDermott, 2012; McDermott & Sokolov, 2009; Salekin et al., 2018). In our experience, defendants are more likely to exaggerate or minimize prior events or symptoms than current mental health symptoms. The clincians's job is to identify the response styles, not the motives for them response styles, but rather when they occur. This can be accomplished by considering issues related to response style and carefully examining the data obtained from records, interviews, and test results with an eye for contradictions or inconsistencies across sources.

Do I understand the psychological literature related to adolescent development and the Miller *factors?* The clinician should be familiar with the normative developmental tasks of this period as well as the things that could influence these tasks, such as family, neighborhood/community, gender, ethnic diversity, culture, and sexual orientation. Additionally, in answering this question, the evaluator should consider literature related to the normal adolescent as described in Chapters 2 and 3. The fourth chapter of *Reforming Juvenile Justice: A Developmental Approach* (National Research Council of the National Academies, 2013) provides a concise discussion of factors that impact youth offending, including but not limited to gangs, parental practices, and racial discrimination.

Am I familiar with the factors that may affect desistance from crime for juveniles and adults? The clinician should consider factors beyond the well-known age–crime curve, which depicts how involvement with criminal activity decreases with age. The topic of desistance was discussed in Chapters 2 and 3.

Do I understand the patterns regarding rate and types of misconduct reports for youth who are put in prison at a young age? This question is particularly important when conducting a resentencing evaluation. On the whole, inmates who enter prison at a younger age have a different pattern (number and type) of acquiring infractions than those who enter when older (Cunningham et al., 2008; Kolivoski & Shook, 2016; Kuanliang et al., 2008). Among those who enter prison between the ages of 14 and 20 years, each year of increased age is associated with a 14.5% decrease in prison misconduct (Kolivoski & Shook, 2016). Familiarity with this body of research allows the clinician to put an individual defendant's disciplinary history in context and inform the court as to how it compares to those who entered prison at an older age.

Am I aware of the evidence regarding the rate of violent institutional assaults for those who have committed murder? Contrary to what is often portrayed in the media, prisoners convicted of murder commit fewer serious institutional assaults than those convicted of less serious crimes (Sorensen, 2010). The clinician should also be familiar with literature related to serious violent offending while in prison among those convicted of murder and among those serving a terminal (either LWOP or death) sentence (Cunningham et al., 2008; Cunningham & Sorensen, 2006; Sorensen, 2010).

Am I familiar with possible unintended and negative consequences of prior juvenile justice involvement, particularly residential placement? Miller defendants may have previous involvement in the juvenile justice system. While residential placement may be successful for some youth (Cruise et al., 2016), it is also associated with various negative consequences, including increases in mental health needs, levels of victimization, and likelihood of subsequent incarceration (Dierkhising et al., 2014; Lambie & Randell, 2013).

Can I identify juvenile justice sentencing and treatment options that have been empirically shown to be effective, as well as those that are ineffective? In reviewing the defendant's prior treatment, the clinician should consider what interventions have targeted particular symptoms, conditions, or problems. (For more information see Cruise et al., 2016; Henggeler, 2016; Viljoen et al., 2016; Weisburd et al., 2017). Just because the court or probation officer referred a juvenile to a certain type of treatment, the clinician should not assume that the intervention was of a kind that is empirically supported (or even that it was provided). The office of Juvenile Justice and Delinquency Prevention (undated) has a searchable Model Program Guide of treatment options and rates them as effective, promising, or having no effect. A good example is boot camps. In 2003, the U.S. Department of Justice demonstrated that boot camps are an ineffective means of reducing recidivism; also see Meade and Steiner (2010) for a more recent discussion of juvenile boot camps.

Competence: Potential Bias

Clinicians, like anyone, can suffer from a bias blind spot—the tendency to recognize bias in others and not in themselves (Pronin et al., 2002; Zappala et al., 2018). When contemplating a referral, forensic psychologists must consider this, identify how their biases might affect their competence, and take steps to reduce this impact (Specialty Guidelines, 2013, section 2.07). When this is not possible, the clinician should refuse the referral (Brodsky, 2013; Specialty Guidelines, 2013, sections 1.02 and 2.07).

Miller cases involve people who committed heinous violent crimes when they were young. These factors alone may present a source of bias. For example, a clinician might believe no one should be sentenced to life for something they did as a teenager, regardless of the crime. Another might feel a defendant should receive the harshest sentence possible for a heinous crime (i.e., the victim was a young child), regardless of their age when it was committed. Either view can compromise objectivity and make it difficult to consider contrary data. Consequently, it is strongly recommended the clinician with either of these beliefs not accept *Miller* referrals. Other biases to watch for include those related to allegiance effect, confirmation bias, or powerful emotional responses to some aspect of the case (Commons et al., 2012; Edens et al., 2012; Murrie et al., 2013; Neal, 2016; Neal & Grisso, 2014; Zapf et al., 2018).

The juvenile and criminal justice systems are marred with racial and ethnic disparities at many levels, ranging from differences in police contact and arrest rates to differences in the lengths of sentences imposed, including the death penalty (Desai et al., 2012; Glaser et al., 2015; Nellis, 2016). Black youth sentenced in criminal court also receive harsher sentences than White youth (Lehmann, 2018). Clinicians in general, and forensic clinicians specifically, are not immune to racial basis (Maina et al., 2018; Shin et al., 2016; Spector, 2001). More often than not, the defendant and the evaluator will not be of the same race, culture, or ethnicity.

"Bias awareness" refers to "the extent to which people are aware of and concerned about the expression and consequence of their bias" (Perry et al., 2015, p. 76). In a novel study examining racial bias awareness among Whites, those authors found that those who are more aware of their racial bias do more to reduce it and are more aware of subtle racism. In our opinion, bias awareness is related to understanding the importance of intersectionality, as described in Chapter 5.

Bias awareness is highlighted in the third guideline of the APA Guidelines on Race and Ethnicity in Psychology (APA, 2019), which states that "psychologists strive for awareness of their own positionality in relation to ethnicity and race" (p. 9). The guidelines define positionality as

> one's own position or place in relation to race, ethnicity, and other statuses, reflecting the ways in which our status reflects power dynamic related to privilege and oppression. Awareness of positionality requires not only understanding the influence of race and ethnocultural and associated privilege and oppression on worldviews and behaviors for people generally but also applying this to oneself in relationships. (p. 13)

To illustrate, imagine three psychologists, all the same age and gender: psychologist A, a Latinx whose parents are doctors; psychologist B, a Latinx who was born to immigrant parents and was the first person in the family to complete high school; and psychologist C, a White American psychologist whose parents are doctors. Through a positionality lens, one could argue that Psychologist A is afforded more privilege compared to Psychologist B but less privilege compared to Psychologist C. This example demonstrates how positionality is relative and applicable regardless of race or ethnicity. The Guidelines on Race and Ethnicity relate this to practice, stating that "psychologists strive to engage in reflective practicing by exploring how their worldviews and positionalities may affect the quality and range of psychological services they provide" (APA, 2019, p. 23).

The current shortage of psychiatrists (National Council Medical Director Institute, 2017) and the overrepresentation of White American psychologists (Lin et al., 2018) make it likely that the person conducting the *Miller* evaluation will be a White psychologist. The overrepresentation of people of color in the legal system makes it likely that the defendant will not be White. Clinicians contemplating conducting these evaluations are urged to engage in the readings and activities described in the Guidelines on Race and Ethnicity. Additionally, White clinicians should understand the impact and perpetuation of important concepts such as White privilege, White fragility, and microaggressions.

A detailed discussion of the APA guidelines is beyond the scope of this book. However, clinicians conducting *Miller* evaluations should be equally versed in those guidelines as in the Forensic Specialty Guidelines. We urge clinicians to apply the APA's race and ethnicity guidelines to various aspects of their forensic practice and apply the guidelines' concept of cultural humility to their clinical work. The following exemplifies how this can impact practice. Imagine a clinician whose practice is to include the defendant's race or ethnicity in every forensic report. After reading the APA Guidelines on Race and Ethnicity the clinician begins to question the rationale and potential negative consequences (e.g., racial stereotypes and bias) of this routine practice. Then the clinician should consider what others (e.g., Riggs Romaine & Kavanaugh, 2018) have written on this issue. As a result, the clinician's practice could go from including the information in every report to including the information in the body of the report only when relevant.

Communication with the Retaining Party

The referral source for *Miller* evaluations could be the court, the state, or defense counsel. In the first instance, the evaluation is court ordered and neither attorney is the client. Another possibility is that one party requests the evaluation, and the court grants the request and issues an order. In this case, the order is typically for the court's funds to pay for the evaluation. A third possibility is that the court is not informed of the evaluation before it occurs, and other funds are used to pay for the evaluation.

In the second and third scenarios the attorney requesting the evaluation is the retaining party. Be prepared to gather information from the retaining party source about the defendant that goes beyond demographics. Ask the source for a description of the case, the potential sentencing options, and any available information relevant to *Miller* factors. It is also critical to clarify expectations and obtain logistical information about the evaluation process.

Obtaining the Retaining Party's Description of the Case

Ideally, the clinician will have an opportunity to communicate with the retaining party to obtain information about the case. In addition to knowing the name of the judge, the attorneys involved, and the docket number, the clinician should gather the following information.

DEFENDANT'S BASIC DETAILS

This includes name, current age, age at the time of the current offense, where the defendant is currently located, how long the defendant has been in jail and/or prison, and potential sentencing options.

STATUS OF THE CASE AND DESCRIPTION OF THE OFFENSE

Determine if the defendant has been found guilty and if this is a *Miller* (re)sentencing or *de facto* life case. Obtain a description of the behavior associated with the charges. This should include a detailed description of the offense and the role the defendant and any co-defendants allegedly played in committing the crime. Since the account of what occurred before, during, and after the offense may be influenced by the retaining party, this account should not be considered an official source to be relied upon as part of the evaluation. This initial description serves only to familiarize the clinician with some of the basic details.

ANTICIPATED LEGAL CONCERNS/ISSUES

The clinician should learn from the retaining party the most basic issues to be addressed in the local jurisdiction. For example, in some states, irreparable corruption is not applied because the state's laws have rejected LWOP for any criminal court sentencing of juvenile crimes. In states that do apply irreparable corruption, it is helpful to know whether the court's procedure typically hears, as a single process, developmental evidence related to the *Miller* factors as well as information related to irreparable corruption. As noted in Chapter 1, some courts might first hear evidence related to irreparable corruption (eligibility for LWOP) and then, if LWOP is judicially rejected, hear further developmental evidence related to alternative sentences. Knowing this can help structure the discussion with the retaining party and will be helpful later with collecting and organizing one's data to fit the court's typical process for *Miller* cases.

The retaining party should have an idea of a reasonable sentencing option. Ask for this information, as it will sometimes impact one's data collection. For example, imagine a resentencing case in which the retaining party believes that the remaining time to release, once the sentence has been adjusted, might be relatively short. In such case, one is more likely to want to plan to use a tool that produces an estimate of risk of recidivism (in contrast to a case in which release time would be too far into the future to make such a score relevant).

ANTICIPATED CLINICAL/DEVELOPMENTAL CONCERNS

Obtain the retaining party's perspective regarding the defendant's potential clinical and developmental issues. Which aspects of the defendant's life, both before and after the offense, concern the retaining party most? By learning the retaining party's concerns, the clinician can use the data collected later and the empirical literature to place these concerns in proper perspective in subsequent communications with the retaining party.

MILLER FACTORS

Obtain an understanding of the retaining party's perspective of relevant information related to each *Miller* factor. The clinician is not endorsing this perspective and should be aware of both allegiance effect and confirmation bias. Asking the retaining party about the *Miller* factors at this stage, however, serves three purposes. One, it allows the clinician to understand (not endorse) the retaining party's concerns. This is similar to asking the retaining party to describe his or her concerns about the defendant's history. Two, think of the concerns as hypotheses to be considered along with those the clinician generates over the course of the evaluation. When the evaluation is completed and the results are discussed with the retaining party, be prepared to describe how the hypotheses were considered, accepted, or rejected. Three, this discussion can highlight areas in which the retaining party has yet to obtain records or identify potential collateral contacts. Additionally, and especially if it is a resentencing case, the clinician will want to ask about the defendant's behaviors and needs since the offense as they pertain to mental health needs, vocational and employment opportunities, and disciplinary involvement, including any that resulted in additional new criminal charges.

Time Expectations for the Evaluation

Some retaining parties contact clinicians well before the trial, sentencing, or resentencing date is set, while others do so only months in advance. The clinician should ask about the anticipated timeline as it pertains to conducting the evaluation and, if needed, receiving a report and providing testimony. Consistent with Specialty Guideline 3.02 (APA, 2013), clinicians should not accept cases they cannot complete in a timely fashion due to their current caseload.

Clarifying Expectations for the Evaluation

As a routine part of the initial contact with the potential retaining party, the clinician should explain generally how the evaluation is conducted and be prepared to answer questions. The evaluator should indicate that the evaluation consists of an in-depth review of records; interview(s) with the defendant; possible administration of psychological and specialized measures to the defendant; collateral interview(s) with those who raised the defendant or who can provide information about the defendant's development, home life, and environment from childhood until the offense occurred; and interviews with other collateral sources. After collecting and analyzing these data, the clinician will develop a clinical opinion related to the specific referral questions.

While discussing the evaluation process, attorneys might have questions about the administration of particular tests or the identification of potential collaterals. Clinicians should consider several possibilities when responding. The attorneys may be asking because they genuinely do not know and want to understand. They might be asking because they are zealously advocating for the defendant or the state (as they should) and are trying to influence the evaluation process. Or it may be both. Whatever influences such questions, clinicians should resist efforts to influence the evaluation process, as this can undermine their impartiality.

Before accepting the referral, the clinician should explain how the opinions reached in the evaluation will be communicated. When retained by the defense, the clinician should verbally share the results and opinions with the retaining party, who will then determine if it is in his or her client's best interest to proceed with writing a report. The retaining party will decide if the report will be tendered to the court and the opposing counsel—or just to opposing counsel to be used in sentence negotiations or as part of another negotiation.

Attorneys in *Miller* cases are expected to zealously advocate for their clients (American Bar Association, 2019). As part of this advocacy, however, the attorney may make requests that are not consistent with the clinician's ethical standards or specialized forensic guidelines (see later in the chapter for examples). It can be helpful to ask about the reason behind the request because it may be possible to directly address the underlying concern in a way that *is* consistent with good practice. In contemplating a response, the clinician should consider the ethics code, relevant specialty practice guidelines, and how the request could impact the reliability and validity of the data obtained.

The attorney may ask the clinician not to administer a particular test to the defendant as part of the evaluation. It is important that the clinician ask the attorney to explain their concern. Often, this concern reflects a misunderstanding or misuse of the test data. For example, attorneys may be apprehensive about how their client will respond to a particular item on a test such as the MMPI-2-RF. In that case, the clinician will want to explain the proper way of interpreting test responses (Ben-Porath, 2012). Regarding which records to review or which tests to administer, the clinician should consider that during cross-examination, it is not unusual for the opposing counsel to ask a series of "who decided" questions, such as: "Doctor, who decided which records you would review?", "Who decided who you would interview?", and "Who decided which tests you would administer to the defendant?" Clinicians want to be able to say that they made all decisions related to the evaluation process. If not, the clinician's objectivity, credibility, and expertise can be questioned.

Counsel could ask to be present for the evaluation. If the attorney takes this issue to court, the judge could grant the request. Before it goes that far, the clinician should explain that the evaluation will likely take place over many sessions and the need to coordinate schedules with the attorney will probably impose a delay in the evaluation process. Upon hearing this, the attorney may decide he or she does not need to be present. If, however, the clinician determines the attorney can be present during the interview portion, it is important to establish ground rules concerning where the attorney can sit in relation to his client, if the attorney can speak during the interview(s), and when the attorney can request a break. In depositions, as attorneys know, if a question has been asked, the person being deposed answers the question first and then takes the break. Clinicians may want to establish this same rule as it decreases the likelihood that the attorney will influence their client's response. Another option is to record the interview portion of the evaluation, although this may not be feasible in many correctional settings. Sometimes the attorney may request to be present during the test administration. Before agreeing to record the testing portion of the evaluation, consider issues related to copyright, standardization, and reliability of the results (APA, 2007; Lewandowski et al., 2016).

Information about the defendant's thinking, feeling, and behavior is directly relevant to the clinician's reasoning about decisional immaturity, offense context, and irreparable corruption. It may also be tangentially relevant to dependency and rehabilitation prospects. Accordingly, obtaining the defendant's account of the offense is quite important. The absence of this information would limit the clinician's ability to draw informed conclusions about several *Miller* factors.

That notwithstanding, the clinician should be mindful of the defendant's Fifth Amendment right to avoid providing self-incriminating information to the court through the evaluation. Some jurisdictions prevent self-incriminating statements obtained for one purpose to be used at another time and for another purpose, but some do not. These circumstances require special attention by the clinician when arranging for the evaluation.

If the retaining party is the defense attorney, the clinician should explicitly discuss with the attorney whether the clinician should talk to the defendant about the offense. Strategically, a defense attorney presumably would want this topic addressed if the report (assuming one is written) is tendered for a sentencing hearing or is used as a pretrial tool in plea bargain discussions. In the latter case, the defense attorney may want to provide the prosecution with clinical information for each *Miller* factor as an essential tool to argue for a lesser charge or a sentence that falls within a specific range. On the other hand, if the retaining party is the prosecution or if the report is court ordered, then the clinician should ask the defense and the prosecution how they can ensure that this information will be used only for appropriate purposes.

In any of these circumstances, for strategic reasons a defense attorney may not want the clinician to talk to the defendant about the offense. For example, this could be the case if the attorney believes his client has pending or potential issues to be addressed in subsequent appeals or has made a claim of innocence. If the attorney does not want the clinician to discuss the offense with his client, this request should be respected. However, the clinician should inform the attorney that not discussing the offense with the defendant precludes the clinician's ability to provide an informed opinion about some of the *Miller* factors. If the defense attorney nevertheless decides against inquiring about the offense, and if a report is written, the report should indicate that the attorney instructed the clinician not to speak with the defendant about the offense. The implications of this restraint on the opinions reached should be included in the report.

Finally, although the defense attorney may have instructed the clinician to inquire about the offense, the clinician might find that the defendant declines to speak about the offense during the evaluation. This may happen when the defendant claims not to have participated in the offense or for more general reasons (for example, "I just don't want to talk about it"). If this occurs, the clinician should (a) inform the defendant that if the defendant does not provide information about his thinking, feeling, and behavior around the time of the offense, then the resulting report will be less thorough and (b) inform the defense attorney. The attorney may choose to talk to the client about the benefits of talking about the offense as part of the evaluation.

Logistics

When considering accepting a referral, the clinician and retaining party should also discuss contractual and logistical issues such as fee structure, access to the defendant, obtaining records, identifying collateral sources, and the jurisdiction of the case.

FEE STRUCTURE

In developing a fee structure, the clinician should keep in mind that, in terms of specialized knowledge and time needed, *Miller* evaluations are more similar to those for the sentencing phase of a death penalty case than any other type of forensic evaluation. As they are relatively new, the clinician should be prepared to educate the retaining party about the logistics underlying the fee structure. In addition to describing one's expertise, explain the amount of time likely needed for activities, such as reviewing possibly voluminous records, interviewing the defendant (often more than once), administering and scoring tests, interviewing the defendant's parents or guardians, and interviewing other collateral sources, including those who knew the defendant prior to and/or since the offense occurred (Specialty Guidelines, 2013, section 5).

Before agreeing to a flat fee, clinicians may want to consider the many influences over the course of the evaluation that can affect the amount of time required to complete it. For example, the clinician might discover more records to review or additional collateral sources to interview. Finally, as in any forensic evaluation, clinicians should also clarify that they are being compensated for the time involved in conducting the evaluation, not for any specific opinion reached, and they expect to be compensated regardless of their clinical opinion or outcome of the case.

ACCESS TO THE DEFENDANT

Typically, the defendant will be detained and not out on bail. In these situations, the clinician should think of access on two levels: what can be brought into the facility and logistics related to meeting with the defendant. Some facilities require a court order before the clinician can bring anything into the facility, while others may have rules prohibiting items needed to conduct the evaluation. For example, a clinician may take notes or administer tests electronically, but the facility may not allow visitors to bring a laptop. Spiral-bound documents are also often prohibited due to concern that the spiral material could be used as a weapon. If the clinician needs to use materials that are typically not allowed, ask the retaining party to confirm the facility's rules and, if necessary, to obtain a court order specifying that the clinician may be exempted from them.

The clinician also needs to know the protocols for entering the facility and arranging meetings with the defendant. The retaining party might be required to inform the facility that the clinician can have access to the defendant. Sometimes a background check or other paperwork must be completed and processed before access is allowed. Other considerations include what days and times the clinician may see the defendant, whether the defendant will be shackled during the meetings, if the clinician will be the only one in the room with the defendant, and if the clinician and the defendant will be separated by a partition or glass. The clinician should be prepared to explain to the retaining party how shackling or the partition can impact the evaluation process and ask for a judicial order requiring the clinician to have access to the defendant in private, without a partition or shackles. Where prior permission is required, written approval from the appropriate person should be requested and a copy of the letter presented to staff on arrival.

ACCESS TO THE PARENTS/CAREGIVERS

Because of the developmental perspective of these evaluations, the parents/caregivers are an essential source of data. Discuss with the retaining party the logistics of these interviews. It is our preference to conduct these interviews in person as this limits the distractions that the interviewee may have to balance while on the phone and allows the evaluator to access and question nonverbal communications. For example, if the caregiver rolls their eyes or appears uncomfortable in response to a line of questioning, this is missed in a telephone interview. When the evaluation is face to face, the clinician can ask about these responses and this could lead to fruitful information. The desire to conduct an in-person interview should be balanced with the "cost" of the interview for the parents/caregivers. This could include costs associated with getting to the office, parking, childcare, and not working. Consequently, when possible, consider conducting home-based interviews.

OBTAINING RECORDS

The clinician should clarify who is responsible for obtaining records. We recommend the retaining party obtain the records and forward them to the clinician. Well in advance of the first evaluation session, the clinician should inform the retaining party what types of records are typically needed for *Miller* evaluations, such as those related to mental health, medical history, education, vocational training, treatment, social service, employment, and prior interactions with the justice system. These types of records are needed not only for the defendant, but for those whom the defendant grew up with as well. The clinician will want copies of the records related to any time police, paramedics, or the fire department were called to any residence the defendant lived in prior to the offense. The clinician and the retaining party should identify records that exist, those that no longer exist, and how long it will take to get the additional records. When records no longer exist or are not available for some other reason, ask the retaining party for a copy of the communication (e.g., letter or email) they received indicating that fact. Unsuccessful attempts to obtain data should be indicated in a report, if one is written. Finally, although not case specific, ask for a copy of relevant state statutes and case law that the court could use to decide the case.

IDENTIFYING COLLATERAL SOURCES

During the initial communication with the retaining party, the clinician may be able to identify potential collateral sources, although it is likely the list will change over the course of the evaluation process. Prior to contacting a collateral source, the clinician will need to obtain the consent of the retaining party (Specialty Guideline 8.03; APA, 2013). The clinician may also solicit the retaining party's help in obtaining contact information for collateral contacts.

JURISDICTION

Clinicians may receive referrals from lawyers in jurisdictions other than the one in which they normally practice. In this case, assuming the clinician has the necessary expertise, the clinician must find out if it is possible to practice in that jurisdiction. Practicing in a state where one is not licensed presents numerous potential problems, including the potential of ethical or regulatory complaints in the state where the evaluation occurred and/or in the state where the clinician is licensed. Consequences could be as serious as losing one's license entirely.

The websites of most states' professional boards include a link to the rules and regulations. Because one's license is at stake, it is our practice to review the regulations, then contact the state board to check that the version of the rules and regulations found on the website is up to date and to confirm that our interpretation is accurate. File a copy of the rules and regulations and any communication with the board in your case file.

The clinician should have some understanding of how long it could take to satisfy the requirements and convey that information to the attorney. Sometimes, the time it takes to complete the licensing approval process may require the attorney to obtain a continuance or retain a clinician who is already licensed in that state.

Planning the Evaluation

After you have determined that you are competent to accept these referrals, have had an opportunity to communicate with a retaining party about a specific case, and understand the logistics involved, you must decide if, given your caseload, you can accept the case. This final level of contemplation should happen on two levels. Level one relates to time: Can you clinician devote the time needed to conduct the evaluation and possible subsequent activities (e.g., submit a report, travel, prepare for testimony, provide deposition testimony, provide hearing testimony)? The second level relates to the possible emotional impact that conducting the evaluation can have on you. *Miller* cases are like capital cases: The possibility of secondary trauma can be great given the nature of the offense(s) and of the defendant's life and circumstances. If, after deliberation, you choose to decline the referral, you could provide the referral source with guidance on how to identify other clinicians who might be able to accept the referral. On the other hand, if you choose to accept the referral, preparation for the evaluation can begin.

After accepting a case, we recommend that the clinician send an engagement letter to the retaining party that covers topics such as identifying the retaining party, what the clinician's role will be, the specific referral questions, the rate or fee structure, and who is responsible for obtaining records. Additionally, providing a list of the types of records needed for review can help the retaining party identify and gather them.

The next step is to develop a plan or roadmap for conducting the evaluation. The referral questions determine the scope of evaluation process. By the nature of the crime, defendants in a *Miller* evaluation are facing either LWOP, a sentence that will be a lengthy term of years, or a *de facto* life sentence. The *Miller* holding clarified the importance of data relevant to irreparable corruption and the other factors relevant in considering sentencing options. Those requirements drive one's planning for data collection, which will be detailed in Chapter 5. Before considering those details, however, we suggest a few more general points about developing the evaluation plan.

First, the clinician should think of developing the plan akin to a "flexible battery." As more reliable and valid forensic instruments become available, clinicians should utilize them in conducting *Miller* evaluations. Depending on the particulars of the case, the clinician should consider including or omitting any instrument and be prepared to explain the rationale on the stand.

Second, at this stage of planning the evaluation, the clinician has a choice to make regarding reviewing the records before or after conducting the interviews and testing with the defendant and/or any collateral interviews. Often a clinician will want to ask the person being interviewed about information contained in the records. Reviewing the records first limits the number of interviews a clinician needs to conduct with the same person. This is particularly important when the clinician is traveling out of state to conduct the interviews.

Finally, once a decision has been made about when to review the records, a timeline for completing the evaluation should be developed. This includes identifying when to read the records; interview and administer testing to the defendant; score and interpret the testing data; interview parents/caregivers and other collaterals; develop a clinical opinion; discuss the opinion with the retaining party; and, if requested, write a report and testify. In drafting this timeline, the clinician should identify which topics are to be explored in which interview and with whom. Also, the clinician should review the notes from previous interviews in preparation for future interviews to identify topics or clarify information that needs to be explored. The timeline is useful as a starting point for scheduling appointments to conduct interviews, and allows one to manage one's caseload effectively. While the timeline provides structure, however, it is not set in stone. As the evaluation progresses, expect to identify additional data sources such as records or collateral contacts that were not initially apparent.

5 Data Collection

An evaluation conducted to aid the court in sentencing a young person who faces a long period of incarceration should be rooted in the same basic tenets as any forensic mental health assessment (e.g. Ackerman, 2010; Heilbrun, 2001; Heilbrun et al., 2009). The data-collection process described in this chapter reflects those principles while highlighting issues particularly germane to cases involving sentencing or resentencing in criminal court for offenses as juveniles.

This chapter describes specific ways to collect data relevant for *Miller* sentencing or resentencing cases, with sections on records, interviews of the defendant and others, and structured assessment methods. Before considering those specific data-collection issues, the first section offers some general guidance for the data-collection process.

The Process of Data Collection

Data collection in *Miller* evaluations typically follows a predictable sequence, although the process often is dynamic, requiring a return to earlier steps in the process as data accumulate. The process also requires attention to inconsistencies that sometimes arise in the data, as well as questions of the quality of the data one is acquiring. This section describes some of these issues that arise throughout the data-collection process.

Sequence of Data Collection

As with any forensic mental health assessment, the process starts with gathering records. In reviewing them, look for data relevant for *Miller*'s developmental factors. As described later, *Miller* evaluations necessitate reviewing records not only for the defendant, but also pertaining to the defendant's family members and caregivers, as they are explicitly relevant for the dependency factor.

Once records have been reviewed, the next step is to acquire interview and testing data. Plan to meet with the defendant multiple times, focusing primarily on the defendant's perspective on the information related to the dependency or decisional factors, and to acquire initial clinical observations of mental health and intellectual disability symptoms. Then interview relevant family members and collaterals to obtain their perspective. Often this will generate new information and require an additional interview with the defendant. This sequence is suggested for two reasons. First, the evaluator can initiate interviews of family members and collaterals with two sources of data in mind: records and defendant interview(s). Second, subsequent re-interviewing of the defendant offers the defendant an opportunity to explain apparent contradictions between the defendant's version and the one provided by other sources.

Once a good working knowledge of the defendant has been developed, one can use clinical judgment to determine which testing instruments/questionnaires to administer. Following the administration procedure as outlined in each instrument's manual is imperative. Similarly, unless prohibited by the manual, asking defendants to explain some of their responses can be fruitful. Simply asking the defendant, "Tell me what you were thinking when you responded to ______" can yield important new data.

More than Multiculturalism: Intersectionality

According to the Specialty Guideline 2.08 (American Psychological Association, 2013),

> forensic practitioners strive to understand how factors associated with age, gender, gender identity, race, ethnicity, culture, national origin, religion, sexual orientation, disability, language,

> socioeconomic status or other relevant individual and cultural differences may affect and be related to the basis for people's contact and involvement with the legal system. (p. 10)

For the sake of ecological validity, we encourage clinicians to also view the defendant through a lens of intersectionality.

The concept of intersectionality requires the clinician to consider the impact of a person's multiple identities instead of considering the identities in isolation. Discussing the concept of intersectionality, Crenshaw (1989) applied the phrase "the sum is greater than its parts" to people's identities or to the multiple systems (e.g. race, gender, sexuality, economic status) in which they live. Consistent with this, the American Psychological Association's Multicultural Guidelines (2017) ask psychologists "to consider the term multicultural in its broadest conceptualization reflecting current literature that considers contextual factors and intersectionality" (Clauss-Ehlers et al., 2019, p. 233; for additional discussion of intersectionality, see Cole, 2009; Grzanka et al., 2017; Lewis & Grzanka, 2016).

As this body of literature evolves, we believe it is imperative to use an intersectional lens to identify and consider the various aspects of a person's identity that may have contributed to involvement with the legal system. Clinicians should also consider how their own different identities can impact how they relate to and understand those they interview. Race/ethnicity, age, sexual orientation, and socioeconomic status are obvious identity factors to consider, both for the evaluator and the defendant. However, we urge clinicians to identify and consider other relevant aspects of identity. Imagine evaluating a defendant who was homeschooled his entire life. His parents chose to homeschool him in such a way that he rarely associated with youth who were not part of his household. Being homeschooled is part of the defendant's identity. Using an intersectionality approach, consider how being homeschooled may have influenced areas of development and psycholegal factors. It is also important to consider how this aspect of the defendant's identity may have affected the other "obvious" identity characteristics. When conducting an evaluation like this, one should be cognizant of how one's own schooling experience and what one knows about homeschooling may impact one's view of the case and hypotheses one generates.

Data Collection Is a Dynamic Process

Do not expect the data-gathering process to be as linear as with many other types of forensic mental health evaluations. Data obtained at one stage or with one method might raise questions that require "circling back" to seek information not found at an earlier stage. For example, it is common to learn about potentially relevant new records during interviews. When deciding if the new records should be requested, weigh their potential utility against the time it could to take to acquire them.

For example, in a recent case involving *Miller* resentencing, the examiner was conducting an evaluation of a defendant who had been imprisoned for 20 years. During the interview, the defendant described something that his legal team did not know and was not in his prison record. Two years prior, he had cared for a dying inmate who was awaiting compassionate leave. The defendant described the training process the prison provided, which included reading a book, taking a test, and signing a form. The defendant's prison file did not contain supporting documentation. The examiner felt that the documentation could yield data related to the defendant's maturity and rehabilitation potential, so the examiner asked the legal team to search for substantiating documentation. After months of searching, it was located in the dying inmate's file rather than the defendant's file.

Awareness of Inconsistent Data

Accepting the dynamic nature of these evaluations allows the clinician to anticipate potential inconsistencies in information. These inconsistencies or contradictions could occur between an interviewee and records reviewed, across interviewees, across records, and across interviews of the same person. Addressing them requires familiarity with and access to the records during the interviews, and/or following up on the apparent contradiction in subsequent interviews.

For example, while being interviewed for a *Miller* evaluation, a 16-year-old defendant indicated that his mother "occasionally" used illicit drugs. He described a time when he was about 11 years old when the police came to his house because he "couldn't wake" his mother. As they did not have a phone, he went to a neighbor, who called 911. In the interview with his mother, she insisted she could not remember this event and did not use drugs. The evaluator asked the retaining party to obtain copies of police and paramedic records from when the defendant lived at that address as well as the mother's medical records. These confirmed what the defendant said: He could not wake her up, she had consumed a large quantity of an illicit substance, and that was not her first overdose. With these documents and information in hand, the evaluator reinterviewed the defendant's mother to give her an opportunity to explain what was going on in her life when the event occurred, more accurately describe her drug use history, discuss how her drug use impacted her parenting abilities, and provide an opportunity to revisit any topic previously discussed.

Data Organization

Identifying apparent contradictions is an ongoing process that occurs while data are being gathered. Waiting until the data collection is complete deprives the clinician of opportunities to seek clarity via additional interviews or records. It is important for the evaluator to have access to the records, or a summary of them, during interviews to note and address apparent contradictions and complexities.

This requires developing a record organization system that reflects the nuances of the case but is also easily accessible. As records are frequently provided electronically, this can be done easily, as will be discussed in another section of this chapter. Additionally, the clinician should routinely review existing data in preparation for new data-gathering activities. Through this review, apparent contractions and areas in need of further exploration will become apparent.

We recommend developing a system for coordinating data across sources according to these objectives. Notes from one's interviews and record reviews can be transferred to columns relevant for each psycholegal factor. Another method for coordinating data across sources is to use a highlighter to color-code the data such that each color represents a different psycholegal factor.

Awareness of Response Style

During interviews, the evaluator should be cognizant of the interviewee's response style. As in death penalty cases, the defendant and family members in juvenile sentencing and resentencing matters tend to minimize the adversity they have experienced. The clinician should be mindful of this when phrasing questions. For example, asking, "Have you ever been physically abused?" can be less effective than "How did your parents respond when you didn't follow the rules, or they thought you did something wrong?" or "How did your parents treat you when they were upset with you?" Following up with questions about the frequency and severity of what the defendant described (e.g. "How often did that happen?" "Did it leave marks?") can help determine if it rises to the level of physical abuse.

Of course, not all those interviewed will present with a minimizing response style. At the other end of the spectrum are exaggerations or mischaracterizations of past events, sometimes with the intention of creating an impression that the defendant believes will serve to reduce the sentence. Assessment tools are sometimes helpful to identify exaggeration or malingering, as discussed in the section of this chapter on "Structured Assessment Methods."

Special Considerations in *Miller* Resentencing Cases

Depending on how long the defendant has been in prison, *Miller* resentencing cases offer special challenges regarding the availability of relevant data. Collateral sources and guardians may no longer be available, as they may have moved or died. School and mental health records may have been destroyed or facilities may no longer exist. On the other hand, the sources of data relevant to prospects for rehabilitation will be greater in a resentencing case than in a *Miller* sentencing evaluation. The evaluator should expect to review a larger quantity of prison records and have more potential sources to interview who can address aspects of prospects for rehabilitation.

These differences may require the clinician to think more creatively about data sources. If the defendant's caregivers are deceased, the clinician might decide to interview the cousin who spent summers in the home. It is certainly important for the expert to be familiar with police and court records related to the offense. These data sources may also be useful in clarifying the defendant's account of the offense.

Records

Records and historical documents offer an important foundation for *Miller* sentencing and resentencing evaluations. This section offers a classification of records typically sought by evaluators, then describes what the evaluator should anticipate learning from each of those types of records.

Miller evaluations typically draw from five main categories of records:

- Education records
- Medical records
- Mental health and treatment records
- Social service/child welfare records
- Juvenile justice system and police records.

In *Miller* resentencing cases, there are three additional types of records:

- Original sentencing hearing transcripts
- Adult corrections records
- Historical accounts of the community.

Miller explicitly instructed courts to "take into account the family and home environment that surrounds him" (p. 2458). Thus, request and review records related to the family members and home environment. A strong organizational structure is essential to managing the volume and variety of information associated

Table 5.1 A Structure for Organizing Information from Records

Source Include as much detail as possible for reference during interviews	Topic/Issue What should be followed up during the interview	Who Possible collateral sources and contact information	Psycholegal Factor Identify relevant factor
Dr. Jones records pdf page 6	Uncle who lived in the home for the year before the offense who is described as "a drunk"	Caregiver and defendant, ? Uncle	Dependency
10th grade report card, school records pdf, page 10	Why absent 40 days that year?	Defendant & caregiver	Decisional and dependency
Green Acres residential treatment records—sent there 6 months before current case due to a VOP release 3 months before the instant offense	Did clinician know that two months before the offense, defendant was told he was adopted? Why not included in notes?	Dr. Martin (xxx-yyy-abcd)	Dependency and possibility for rehabilitation

with these cases. A chart like the one in Table 5.1 can help during review, interview preparation, interviews, and follow-up.

Education Records

Academic records can provide information about a youth's cognitive functioning and behavior within the educational system, sometimes relevant for the decisional, dependency, and potential for rehabilitation factors. Educational records can also provide information related to family functioning and are a potential source for identifying collaterals to interview. They can also provide insight on family functioning. In some cases, educational records of family members are also relevant. For example, it might be useful to review documentation (educational or disability records) of a parent's limited cognitive abilities and adaptive functioning. This information could relate to the parent's ability to care for and supervise the defendant.

COGNITIVE FUNCTIONING AND BEHAVIOR

Many youth in the juvenile justice system receive special education services. Familiarity with the process for obtaining and maintaining special education services is important when conducting these evaluations. Burrell and Warboys (2000) provide a concise explanation of this process as it applies to the juvenile justice system. Schools perform assessments and develop plans called individualized education programs (IEPs) to determine eligibility for special education services. If the youth is eligible, then an IEP reassessment occurs every three years, or sooner if requested by the parents or teacher. If a student was evaluated for or receives special education services, the educational records should contain documents related to the initial IEP evaluation or renewal evaluation process. The documents include a social history typically produced by a social worker based on interviews with the student (and, ideally, the caregiver) and a psychological evaluation containing a developmental assessment along with the results of cognitive and academic assessments.

These documents may contain information that can be used to compare the defendant's abilities to other youth of similar age. In some cases, the psychological report will also contain an assessment of mental health needs or issues. In some jurisdictions these initial or renewal records may be kept separately from behavioral, attendance, and grade transcripts. When this is the case, a specific request for these other records may be needed.

Approximately 85% of youth in the juvenile justice system are eligible to receive special education services, but only a third receive those services (National Council on Disability, 2015). This suggests that many of the education records reviewed will describe a student who had unidentified special education needs.

FAMILY FUNCTIONING IN EDUCATION RECORDS

Educational records can provide useful contemporaneous data about family functioning. Consider what is present as well as what is missing. For example, the records could contain letters or notations documenting unsuccessful attempts to reach parents, and failure of caretakers to attend IEP meetings. The records could also contain a summary of interactions between school officials and the defendant's primary caregiver. If so, the evaluator could inquire about these things during interviews with the caregiver and the defendant to gain a better understanding of how the family functioned at that time. When reviewing school records, close attention should be paid to changes in grades or behavior, and the caregivers and defendant can be asked what was going on in their lives at that time.

IDENTIFYING POTENTIAL COLLATERALS TO INTERVIEW

Teachers can be useful sources for collateral interviews. For example, during one *Miller* evaluation, the defendant's former teacher shared that the family had moved frequently. The defendant chose not to change schools, resulting in a 90-minute commute on public transportation each way. She recalled the defendant frequently was dressed inappropriately for the weather. Once she gave him a blanket so he could keep warm as he waited for the bus. He returned it the next day, explaining, "My mom said I can't keep it because I don't need another mother."

A situation like the one just described can yield important insights about family dynamics and suggest additional directions for interviews with the defendant and caregivers. With the defendant, the clinician may ask about the impact of the family's frequent moves, why he chose not to switch to a closer school, what role the teacher played in his life, and what thoughts and feelings he had when his mother told him he could not have the blanket. His mother could explain what prompted the moves. Were they related to financial instability, substandard housing, drug use by a resident of the apartment, or threat of eviction? She could be asked why she told her son to return the blanket. What did it mean to her that the teacher had given it to him?

Medical Records

DEFENDANT'S MEDICAL RECORDS

As it pertains to the defendant, these records may contain information that could impact cognitive and psychosocial development such as head traumas or gunshot wounds. A professional's observations related to the defendant's comprehension and cognitive abilities may also be found in these records. As always, the clinician should look for gaps. For example, are any years missing for annual physicals? If so, inquiry is warranted because it may provide useful information about family norms, beliefs, expectations, and resources.

Records from overnight hospitalizations or emergency room visits can be particularly fruitful. Nursing records may include who visited or stayed overnight with the defendant. It is noteworthy, for example, if the defendant spent three nights in the hospital for an emergency procedure and the only mention of caregiver presence is related to discharge planning. If an older aunt visited multiple times, she might be able to provide data related to the family functioning at that time as well as more details regarding why the defendant was hospitalized. Discharge notes may identify sources that house other relevant records that might need to be requested.

CAREGIVERS' MEDICAL RECORDS

We recommend seeking not only the defendant's medical records, but also those of caregivers. The latter can sometimes reveal medical factors that limited the caregiver's ability to meet the defendant's needs (sometimes relevant for the dependency factor).

Caregivers' medical records are helpful for two reasons. They can provide a picture of challenges the caregiver faced due to managing medical, sometimes chronic, conditions. For example, imagine discovering during an interview with a grandmother who has been the defendant's caregiver that she is being treated for diabetes and high blood pressure, both potentially life-threatening conditions. Records include multiple notations about lack of compliance with the medical regimen. Pursuing this issue during interviews could yield important data not documented elsewhere related to *Miller* questions.

Reviewing caregivers' medical records can also reveal periods of parental absence. These absences may be relatively short, as in the case of an emergency room visit, or could be longer, such as a stay in a hospital followed by time in a rehabilitation facility or a parent's incarceration. In the interviews it is important to explore how these absences impacted family functioning—ranging from how basic needs were met to how the defendant was supervised. This discussion could also provide context for other areas in the defendant's life such as performance at school or school attendance as well as juvenile justice or social service involvement. For example, if the clinician learns from the mother's medical records that she had a stroke when the defendant was 15 years old, the clinician could ask the defendant specifically about this period of his life. The clinician may learn that this event coincides with the 15 consecutive days he was absent from school that year because he stayed home to care for a younger sibling. Since it was at the end of the month, when family funds were low, he stole food for them to eat. Bear in mind, though, that the youth's resourcefulness should not automatically be equated with maturity.

Medical records of others who live in the household might be useful. Imagine reviewing the dental records for the defendant's younger sister describing the time when she was five and the defendant was 14 years old, two years before the instant offense. Her records reveal that most of her teeth were decaying. This should raise questions for the clinician related to the dependency factor, such as whether the decay was the result of neglect or of a medical condition. If it was the former, then this should raise additional important questions. What type of parenting did the defendant receive during this time in his life? How were his basic needs addressed? Who supervised him? How did the family function during this time? These questions should be posed to both the caregiver and the defendant.

Mental Health and Treatment Records

The defendant's mental health records, including outpatient, inpatient, drug and alcohol treatment, and family treatment, often provide information related to all of the *Miller* factors. The evaluator should attend to what precipitated a given intervention, what the intervention was intended to address, who participated, rate of attendance, and professional impressions, including diagnosis. Equally important are comments related to the home environment, including who was living in the home and how the family was functioning. These records are important because they might or might not provide contemporaneous support of the historical accounts or "memories" interviewees provide.

These records could contain data related to the dependency and prospects for rehabilitation factors. For example, depending on the biological caregiver's diagnosis, there could be a genetic predisposition relevant to the defendant's treatment needs as they relate to the prospects for rehabilitation factor. In some cases, the defendant or family members may not have mental health or treatment records. In such cases, examiners should consider the possibility of unmet needs.

Social Service, Child Welfare, and Foster Placement Records

These records are particularly important as they often provide information related to the dependency factor, especially regarding abuse, trauma, and neglect. The records should be requested for those living in the defendant's household from the time the defendant was a child through the time of the offense. Reviewing records of the defendant's siblings could also provide useful information.

Requesting the social service or child welfare records for the caregivers when they themselves were children could also yield useful information. For example, they could shed light on generational factors that were beyond the defendant's control but possibly influencing his treatment needs or risk for criminal behavior.

Clinicians should not equate the absence of social service records with the absence of abuse, trauma, or neglect in the defendant's childhood or adolescence. It is not unusual to learn about abuse and neglect that should have been brought to the attention of authorities but was not.

Juenile Justice, Police and Criminal Justice Records

Information relevant for all of the *Miller* factors often is provided by records from the juvenile justice system. These will include (a) juvenile court records regarding the youth's legal processing on past delinquency charges, (b) records from probation officers for past periods of juvenile probation, and (c) records from juvenile correctional programs if the youth has previously been in juvenile corrections.

The review of these records should go far beyond what is available in the criminal history summary. Whenever possible, it should include as many first-hand documents (police report, witness statements, and the like) as possible—describing the circumstances, nature, and outcome of each offense. For example, if a defendant was placed on probation, the probation records should be reviewed. If those records reveal that while on probation the youth was sent to corrections or to a residential facility, records from those out-of-home placements should also be reviewed. Imagine one of these documents indicates that the defendant at age 13 witnessed a shooting at 2 a.m. miles away from his residence. This raises questions to explore with the defendant, caregiver, and possibly other collateral interviewees. Why was the youth allowed outside at that time of the morning? Did the youth leave with caregiver's permission? If not, did the caregiver simply feel tired after multiple attempts to convince the youth to stay home to no avail?

Probation, court, and corrections records sometimes provide information about a defendant's victimization. Such information is important because of known relationships between victimization and future offending (Shaffer & Ruback, 2002) and to identify possible mental health needs potentially related to prospects for rehabilitation.

Juvenile justice and police records are important sources of information for evaluating the offense context factor. They often provide an "official" account of the offense, witness accounts, and descriptions of the defendant's behavior around the time of the offense. At minimum, these records should include an original police document related to the offense, arrest, and interrogation.

When an interrogation has been recorded, the clinician should review the recorded version as well as the transcript. The recorded version may contain important information about the defendant's demeanor or abilities (e.g., auditory comprehension) that are not apparent in the transcript. Recordings made close in time to the offense may contain information related to the offense context factor. For example, imagine a scenario where the defendant alleges he was intoxicated at the time of the offense. The police began interrogating him within an hour of the offense occurring. His behavior during the interrogation may be useful as it relates to the issue of intoxication, but this may not be reflected in the transcript.

When conducting an evaluation where the defendant has already been adjudicated, it is important to review portions of the trial transcripts because they may contain valuable information related to any of the *Miller* factors. It is not unusual for defense counsel to introduce mitigation evidence during the trial. When this occurs, that portion of the transcript should be reviewed carefully. For example, the defendant or others (e.g., witnesses to the offense, co-defendants in the offense) may have testified about the offense. A review of that testimony could yield valuable information for the offense context analysis.

Additional Records Relevant for Resentencing Cases

Records that are relevant for resentencing cases specifically include transcripts of original sentencing hearings, adult corrections records, and historical information about community variables.

RECORDS OF ORIGINAL SENTENCING HEARINGS

In resentencing cases, one should review the original sentencing hearing transcript. It may contain witnesses' or judicial perspectives of data related to the *Miller* factors. In one resentencing case, the transcript of the original sentencing included the judge's discussion of the hardships in the defendant's life, the defendant's role in the offense, and the defendant's immaturity, yet the judge stated he had no choice but to sentence the defendant to life without parole (LWOP).

ADULT CORRECTIONS RECORDS

The review of the defendant's disciplinary records during adult correctional incarceration includes a list of infractions but goes beyond numbers and types to reviewing the actual disciplinary "write-ups." Often these are written by a correctional officer, describing the circumstances of the infraction event. Infraction history should be reviewed in detail with the defendant so the clinician can obtain the defendant's perspective of contextual details of infractions beyond what is documented in the records. To prepare for that portion of the interview, when reviewing the disciplinary records, the clinician should make note of when during the course of incarceration the offense occurred, the level of infraction (often infractions are rated major or minor), what occurred, the pattern (type and frequency) of infractions over the course of the incarceration, and the outcome of each infraction. Sometimes behavior that is labeled a minor infraction at one time is labeled as major another time. This may necessitate asking the retaining party to obtain prison documents explaining why this occurred.

Apart from records of individual infractions, correctional staff often are required periodically to complete a form that rates an inmate's risk for escape and/or security threat level. Often this document is completed annually and used to determine where the inmate is housed. A low or medium risk and/or threat level could result in the inmate being placed in a lower-level security tier or institution. However, in these cases, this is often overridden because the inmate is sentenced to LWOP. This provides clinically valuable information regarding how the prison officials viewed the inmate, which could contribute to analysis of the prospects for rehabilitation factor.

The review of the defendant's work history should go beyond the list of jobs held. It should also include requests the defendant made to obtain work that were denied and the reason they were denied. For example, was it because all the positions were filled? Because the inmate was not perceived as qualified? Because the length of his sentence prevented him from working in that position? The records may also contain information about the supervisor's impression of the inmate's work. In some jurisdictions, prison supervisors routinely review inmates' work and rate them on qualities such as attendance, ability to get along with others, and how they perform the tasks of the job. These documents could shed light on the prospects for rehabilitation factor as well any changes over time to the decisional factor. Prison work records are also a good source for identifying prison personnel to interview as collateral contacts.

Prison mental health records should be examined. According to the U.S. Department of Justice (Bronson & Berzofsky, 2017), the prevalence of mental health problems is greater in prison than in the community at large. (See Prins, 2014, and Gottfried & Christopher, 2017, for a review.) Despite this, many inmates with a mental illness do not receive treatment while in prison (Bronson & Berzofsky, 2017; Reingle et al., 2014). Only about one-third of the inmates who need mental health services receive them (Bronson & Berzofsky, 2017). As evaluators, we have heard from inmates that unless the needs are severe, seeking mental health services could make an inmate vulnerable to being preyed upon. Obviously, this will vary from facility to facility and defendant to defendant. The absence of significant mental health records does not mean there was not a mental health need, however. The possibility of unmet mental health needs should be considered when evaluating the defendant.

Research suggests a relationship between inmate mental health needs and institutional write-ups. According to the U.S. Department of Justice, inmates with mental health problems are more likely to be written up for assaulting a correctional officer or another inmate than those without mental health problems (Bronson, 2017). When reviewing the mental health records, the clinician should consider any possible relationship between disciplinary write-ups and notations of receiving mental health service or potential unmet mental health needs (e.g., notations of odd behavior). Using a program such as Excel, PowerPoint, or Keynote could help the pattern emerge visually.

When reviewing the records, the clinician should make note of any programming other than paid work in which the defendant was involved or attempted to obtain. This information is relevant to the prospects for rehabilitation factor. Programming could vary and include educational activities (such as obtaining a GED or taking classes led by community volunteers), substance abuse treatment, anger management, and parenting or technology classes. Sometimes upon completion of the class, the inmate is given a certificate that is kept in the prison file. In some institutions, serving an LWOP sentence limits the types and number of programs available to the inmate. It is, however, important to have a grasp of the programming opportunities prior to discussing this with the defendant.

An acronym frequently seen in prison records is "STG" (Security Threat Groups). It is used when prison officials determined that at some time the inmate was gang-involved. If the records indicate STG, it is important to find out what, in this particular case, led to this label being assigned. Was it because the crime committed 20 years ago was gang-related? Does it reflect something that occurred while in prison? Prior to discussing this with the defendant, ask the retaining party to provide documentation describing the process for removing the STG label. Often, this involves a renouncing process that could make the inmate vulnerable to being attacked by the gang being renounced—regardless of whether the inmate was actually in the gang. The impact of the STG label and decision to engage (or not) in the renouncing process should be explored in the interview with the defendant. More information on STG and the renouncing process can be found on the National Institute of Corrections (2017) website.

Finally, prisons have an internal investigation department (the name of which varies from facility to facility). If an inmate has been investigated by this department, the documentation is typically not in the inmate's file but is kept in a separate file in the internal investigation department. This separate file must be specifically requested. It is important that the retaining party requests this file as it could contain data relevant to the prospects for rehabilitation factor. In one case, documentation that explained why the inmate was transferred to a facility out of state was in the internal investigation file, not the inmate's general prison file. The inmate prevented a guard from being assaulted and was transferred to prevent retaliation. The documentation corroborated the defendant's explanation for the transfer, which would not have been possible without seeking the records from this internal investigation file.

HISTORICAL COMMUNITY PROFILES

Resentencing cases often will revisit the original offense and the factors that may have led to the defendant's involvement in criminal activity as a juvenile. Part of that analysis involves understanding the community in which the offense occurred. Community factors (e.g., poverty, drugs, violence, and crime) where the defendant grew up, and where the crime occurred, may have changed with time. The likelihood of this occurring increases with the duration of the defendant's incarceration. Impartial sources such as newspaper articles and/or government reports that describe conditions when the defendant was in the community can aid the expert as well as the court.

For example, during 15 years of incarceration, the projects where one defendant grew up were torn down and replaced with very expensive single-family homes. An internet search led to newspaper articles and government documents describing the poverty, crime, and gang activity during the time the defendant lived there. Historical documents describing communities are helpful for several reasons: to corroborate information obtained via interviews, to obtain data related to the dependency factor, and to remind the evaluator and the court of the conditions where the defendant lived prior to the adjudicated offense. If the "how things were" documents are useful, the clinician should consider attaching them as an appendix to the report.

Interviews with Defendants

When conducting the interviews, evaluators should keep two things in mind. First, it is possible to challenge the interviewee in a manner that does not negatively impact the working relationship between the clinician and the interviewee. Second, use the "close your eyes" test. This involves collecting enough details so that you can close your eyes and see how things unfolded from the interviewee's perspective. If you have to make assumptions, you have not asked enough questions. While this may result in the interviews taking longer, it can yield more useful data and allows clinicians to consider how their own biases may be distorting the data.

Begin interviewing the defendant, provide a notification. Textbooks such as Melton et al. (2018) and Heilbrun et al. (2014) indicate that the notification should include the following elements:

- the purpose for the evaluation, including the legal issue at hand
- who asked for the evaluation
- your role in the case
- the limits of confidentiality
- who gets a copy of the reports
- clarification of the defendant's role.

A notification in a *Miller* sentencing or resentencing case might look like this:

Given regardless of who is the retaining party: Hello, I am Dr. X. The judge/your attorney/the state asked that I evaluate you to gather information that the court could consider before (re)sentencing you.

If retained by the judge: I will write a report based on what I have learned. The report can include anything you tell me. The judge, the prosecutor, and your attorney will get a copy of the report. If I testify, I can repeat anything you have told me in court.

If retained by the defense or prosecution: I will use the information you provide and that I collect to develop my clinical opinion. I will share that opinion and anything you tell me with the (insert retaining party). If they decide that they want me to write a report, I will. I can include anything you tell me in the report. The judge, prosecutor, and your attorney will get a copy of the report if the report is used as evidence. If I testify, I can repeat anything you have told me in court.

Given regardless of who is the retaining party: I will be asking you a lot of questions. I do that because I want to understand your perspective and don't want to make assumptions about your experiences. We can take a break whenever you want. All you have to do is ask. It is important that you answer my questions as honestly and accurately as possible. For example, I might ask about information in your school, court, or jail records because I want to see if you agree with the way situations were described. If I say something that you don't understand or doesn't make sense, please let me know. At some point I will be administering tests. It is important that you do your best on the tests because I could let the court know how you performed on those tests as well.

As indicated in Chapter 4, the clinician should know if it is permissible to talk to the defendant about the offense prior to beginning the evaluation, If the retaining party has advised the clinician not to discuss the offense with the defendant, the notification should include a statement such as: "We will not be talking about the offense." When the clinician is permitted to talk to the defendant about the offense, the notification should include something like this:

> At some point we will be talking about the offense. When we get to that part of the evaluation, I am going to be asking you a lot of questions. Again, my questions are because I want to understand things from your perspective, what happened, and what you were thinking and feeling as they happened.

Finally, it is important that the clinician take the time necessary to ensure that the defendant understands the notification, sometimes by asking the defendant to explain what things mean. The clinician should document the defendant's understanding in writing and include this information in the report, if one is requested.

Interview Process

Several meetings with the defendant to gather interview information typically are required. In part, this is due to the sheer amount of information involved. It also provides time to follow up on data as they are acquired and ask about any inconsistences. The clinician might also need to ask about the defendant's responses to the tests administered. As indicated earlier in this chapter, the examiner must be aware of defendants' potential tendencies to report in a manner that serves their own interests, requiring appropriate inquiry to challenge such things if they arise. The following sequence is recommended for defendant interviews: (a) social developmental history; (b) dissecting the offense; (c) personal view of prospects; and (if it is a resentencing evaluation) (d) life in prison.

Social/Developmental History

This portion of the interview with the defendant should be like those described in standard forensic texts. Use the interview to obtain the defendant's own account and recollections of family and social history, substance use treatment and needs, mental health treatment and needs, trauma, and personal development.

VALUE OF ANCHORED INTERVIEWING

Miller explicitly recognized that community and family can be a source of negative influence on a youth and urged the court to consider this when rendering an individualized sentence. Accordingly, the clinician should anchor the inquiry of the developmental history within the defendant's family and community context. Track the defendant's history so that you can compare it to those of similar ages. We have found that youthful defendants have an easier time providing their history in a sequential, chronological fashion when asked about school or where they lived, as opposed to using specific years. Defendants may not be able to remember the year that something occurred, but often they can remember what school they attended or where they lived. Using these as anchors, the clinician can inquire about who lived in the residence(s) when the defendant attended the certain school or vice versa. This should be done in addition to, not in lieu of, gathering the typical social developmental history. The benefit of such anchoring is that it helps the clinician become aware of significant changes in the defendant's life that the defendant might not appreciate or spontaneously disclose. The following hypothetical example demonstrates how this anchoring process can work.

Early in the interview, the clinician asked the defendant to generate a list of all the schools she attended. Then the clinician asked the defendant to recall where she lived when she attended each school, keeping in mind that often youth have lived at more than one address when they attended a particular school. Next, the clinician might ask the defendant to try to recall who lived with her in each residence. As it is not unusual for defendants to spontaneously recall only the primary caregiver, be prepared to prompt the defendant to think of anyone else who lived in the residence at that time.

Keep these lists available for reference as data are collected. If the defendant describes a year in which her grades and behavior changed at school, the lists might show that those living with the defendant also changed around that time. For example, by asking the defendant to explain why her mother only lived with her for "about half the year," the defendant could explain that this was the year that her mother went to jail. Using the "close your eyes" test, this should lead the clinician to ask a series of questions ranging from what the defendant knows now and knew then about when and why her mother was arrested, how her mother's absence was explained to her at the time, and how she felt about the absence to asking the defendant if she thinks there might be a connection between what was going on at home, who cared for her and how that person(s) treated her, and how she was acting at school. This series of questions can yield data related to dependency psycholegal factor.

Using the list as anchors, the clinician should inquire about the neighborhoods where the defendant lived to obtain information related to poverty, safety, and crime. Likewise, gather information about each person who lived in the residences over the course of the defendant's life. This inquiry should include the defendant's relationship with the person (e.g., how they felt about the person, if they could confide in the person, if and how they were disciplined by the person). Ask about the possible criminogenic factors for each person who lived in the household or with whom the defendant associated. For defendants who were gang-involved or who engaged in previous criminal activities, ask what the defendant thought or understood about these activities at that time—and how the person(s) with whom the defendant lived responded to these activities. Similarly, if a person in the household used drugs or alcohol, ask what the defendant thought about this behavior at that time. To the degree that the person was playing the role as a primary caregiver, it is important to find out if there were periods when that person was not available. If so, who took that role during those times?

BEYOND FACTS: THE DEFENDANT'S PERSPECTIVE

The description of the interview with the defendant has focused on gathering factual data about the defendant's childhood and adolescence, but the interview can serve two other important purposes. One is to understand the defendant's perspective on the family environment and community across time, and to use the interview to gain information about the defendant's psychosocial development at various stages. As factual data are being collected, inquire about the defendant's personal thoughts and feelings about those matters. Explore both the defendant's perceptions of the circumstances at the time and the defendant's perspective now, looking back on the circumstances. The other purpose is to gather data assessing the defendant's decisional capacities or tendencies and psychosocial development at various points in the defendant's history, as well as the defendant's psychosocial development now as the defendant reflects on the past.

For example, ask a youthful defendant to describe a time when something did not go as planned. Use this instance as an anchor and ask questions aimed at gathering information related to different aspects of psychosocial development such as who was involved, what role peer influence may have had, what was the goal of the event, what risks or downsides were (or were not) considered at the time, and what future orientation was involved at the time. Then ask the defendant to examine the event from where the defendant sits now: "Okay, so you described something that happened two years ago. Now, looking back on it, I want to ask you some questions." Then ask questions related to psychosocial development. This provides information to assess how, if at all, the individual has changed from a psychosocial perspective.

Such questions are especially important in resentencing cases where more time has passed between adolescence and the defendant's current stage of development. A further important benefit of this level of inquiry is that it prepares the defendant for another crucial part of the interview focusing on the offense.

Dissecting the Offense

Unless otherwise instructed by the retaining party, the clinician should use the interview with the defendant to obtain a detailed understanding of the offense. This is not unusual for forensic mental health professionals. This type of retrospective inquiry is expected when the legal issue involves a reconstructive consideration of mental state (e.g., an insanity defense). Like other retrospective inquiries, it involves gaining an understanding of the days leading up to the offense, the circumstances surrounding the offense itself, and possibly extending beyond. However, when conducting a developmentally sensitive *Miller* evaluation, this inquiry takes on a broader scope. The clinician seeks understanding, from the defendant's perspective, about the role the defendant played in offense, how the defendant's family or peers may have contributed to the defendant's involvement, and what the defendant was (or was not) thinking as the events unfolded. This inquiry results in data related to the decisional, dependency, and offense context factors.

During this part of the interview, explore the level of forethought or premeditation involved from a developmental perspective. One defendant saying to another "Let's do a crime" might connote intent, but by itself it does not suggest a plan. To appraise the degree of planning more carefully, the clinician should ask a series of questions to gauge the level of appreciation for the risk and rewards the defendant had at the time of the offense and the level of discussion about the details of who would do what as the crime unfolded, and what would happen in the aftermath.

The following provides an example of the benefits of conducting a developmentally sensitive interview and applying the "close your eyes" test. In the initial exploration, the defendant, Mark, tells you that days before the robbery, which resulted in a death, the defendants, both 16 years old, discussed the crime. When asked to describe the discussion, the following exchange occurred:

Clinician: Tell me about what you guys discussed, talked about.
Mark: I said to Johnny, "Do you want to go and break into Mr. Max's house to get money so we can go to the concert?"
Clinician: What did he say?
Mark: "Yeah, man."

Without appropriate developmental inquiry the above could be interpreted to represent a plan reflecting developed thinking. A more developmentally appropriate inquiry might include the following:

Clinician: Did you discuss how you were going to break into the house?
Mark: Yes.
Clinician: Tell me about that conversation.
Mark: We said, "We will take a brick with us."
Clinician: Did you discuss what you guys would do with the brick, or who would use it?
Mark: No.
Clinician: Did you talk about if Mr. Max might be home?
Mark: No.
Clinician: Did Mr. Max live with anyone?
Mark: Yeah, I think he is married. I don't know.
Clinician: Did you talk about what you would do if Mr. Max or his wife were home?
Mark: No.
Clinician: You said you wanted to break into his house to get money to go to a concert.
Mark: Yes.

> *Clinician*: Where was the concert?
>
> *Mark*: Two towns over.
>
> *Clinician*: How far is that?
>
> *Mark*: If you drive about an hour, I guess. I am not sure.
>
> *Clinician*: Did either one of you have a car or have access to a car?
>
> *Mark*: No.
>
> *Clinician*: Did you have a ride to the concert?
>
> *Mark*: I don't know.
>
> *Clinician*: Okay, I want to make sure I understand what you are saying. The idea was to break into the house to get money to go to a concert? Do I have it right?
>
> *Mark*: Yes.
>
> *Clinician*: And the concert was about an hour away by car?
>
> *Mark*: Yes.
>
> *Clinician*: But you didn't have a ride?
>
> *Mark*: Right.
>
> *Clinician*: Could you take public transportation to get there?
>
> *Mark*: No, I don't know. I have never done that.
>
> *Clinician*: Okay, help me understand how you were going to get to the concert.
>
> *Mark*: I didn't think about it. I was just happy that we were going to be able to go.

This provides useful information on the nature and extent of the planning.

Asking about the defendant's perception of the offense's impact can sometimes yield information about the defendant's sense of empathy as well. Does the defendant's description of how he felt right after the offense suggest only concern for himself, or something more? In one case, when the clinician asked the defendant what he did right after the fight in an alley in which he stabbed a man, he said, "I ran home." When asked if he checked to see how badly the man was hurt before he ran, he said no. Asked what he was thinking about while running home, he said that on the way he decided to stop at an acquaintance's house and call 911 to report that "a man is down" and gave the location of the alley. (Later review of 911 records confirmed that such a call was made at the relevant date and time.)

In retrospect, at the time of the interview, can the defendant identify how the offense affected the victim's family, the neighborhood, or the community? It is useful to ask open-ended questions such as "What was the impact of the murder?" Regardless of how the defendant responds, encourage the defendant to provide other examples of the impact. The response of a 17-year-old defendant may evolve from "It got me locked up" to the same defendant 20 years later, "Now the kids don't have a father and that is wrong." The defendant might elaborate, "Those poor kids, they don't have a father. One was just a baby and really never got to know his dad. Since I broke into the house in the middle of the night, I am sure people were afraid when they went to sleep that someone could break into their house and hurt them."

Dissecting the offense also involves asking defendants to share their thoughts and feelings about their role in the offense. One might assume that this will not be useful because the response will be self-serving, but there may be important variations and nuances relevant to the *Miller* factors discussed in this book. We have had one resentencing case in which, years after the offense, the defendant stated that he did not feel badly about committing the offense and could only identify how the offense impacted him and his family. By contrast, in a different resentencing case in which the defendant killed two people (an innocent bystander and opposing gang member), the defendant described why he regretted killing the innocent bystander. However, 30 years after the offense, he voiced conflicting feelings about killing the opposing gang member. He continued to feel that what he did was right because, just as he thought at the time, he felt they were "at war." On the other hand, he was now able to discuss how, with time, he realized that not everyone lived by those rules.

In addition to the Fifth Amendment issues previously described, dissecting the offense offers different challenges in sentencing and resentencing cases. Most *Miller* sentencing evaluations will be conducted pre-adjudication. Often it is difficult for a defendant to talk about the offense honestly or in the depth required before the defendant has been found guilty. Acknowledging or "giving voice" to this potential challenge may aid in increasing the defendant's ability to provide the level of detail needed and to tolerate the inquiry. Use clinical judgment to determine when to provide the acknowledgment, which could look like this:

> At some point during this evaluation we are going to talk about the offense. I want to learn what was going on from your perspective when the offense occurred. I know that might seem strange because the court hasn't said you are guilty of the crime. But it is important that this evaluation is conducted before the court makes that decision. If the court determines that you are not guilty, then the court won't need the report. If the court decides that you are guilty, then the information in the report could help the court understand what was going on from your perspective when the offense occurred. The idea is that the court would consider this information before sentencing you. So, talking about the offense with me gives you a chance of making sure the judge understands things from your perspective if you are found guilty.

Resentencing evaluations pose a different potential challenge. Our experience is that prisoners learn to navigate prison or "do their time" by not talking about their offense with other inmates and certainly not talking about it with the level of detail required for this evaluation. Therefore, the process of describing the offense may be difficult or a source of anxiety for the defendant. It is important that defendants not return to their cell feeling vulnerable or overwhelmed, as this has an impact on their welfare on many levels. Because of the difficulty involved in discussing the offense in the necessary detail, be prepared to discuss the offense in two separate interviews, each time ending the interview by discussing something unrelated to the offense.

Dissecting the offense in a resentencing evaluation also involves obtaining information about how the defendant currently thinks and feels about the offense and the defendant's role in it. This can be accomplished by asking "From where you sit now, as a grown man/woman, what do you think about X or Y?" Using the example provided earlier, the clinician might ask, "Looking back on it, how do you feel about committing a robbery that turned into a murder to get money to go to a concert?" Thirty years after the offense, the defendant might respond, "It was stupid." When asked why it was stupid, the defendant might say, "We weren't thinking. What were we going to do with the money? How were we going to get to the concert, walk? We had no plan." Asking the defendant to look at the offense from a current perspective can provide data related to the defendant's growth and maturity over time.

Defendant's View of Prospects for Rehabilitation

This portion of the interview is very different for a resentencing versus a sentencing evaluation. In the former, you are inquiring about how defendants "did their time" and the choices they made while incarcerated. This involves, but is not limited to, obtaining the defendant's perspectives on disciplinary reports, involvement (or lack thereof) in mental health services, work history, and program involvement. For example, if the defendant has been involved in anger management, substance abuse, and parenting groups, the clinician should learn why the defendant chose to participate in these activities considering the sentence was LWOP. On the other hand, if the defendant's prison records reflect the absence of participation in programming, the clinician should inquire about this as well.

In our experience, in some jurisdictions, LWOP prisoners may not have access to many aspects of programming because others without life sentences are given priority. If the defendant's records do not indicate participating in services or programs, the clinician may want to investigate the feasibility of LWOP inmates participating. Having this knowledge in advance allows the clinician to have a better understanding of the accuracy of the information the defendant provides. Sometimes LWOP inmates may respond that they are not allowed to participate. In actuality, the prison policy may be that LWOP inmates are allowed but those who do not have life sentences have priority for participating. As a portion of this inquiry (e.g., discussing disciplinary reports and work history) is tied to the records, having the records at hand is helpful. Finally, as part of this inquiry, ask defendants to explain how they have changed while in prison.

While the inquiry regarding the prospects in a resentencing case is primarily retrospective, a *Miller* sentencing evaluation is primarily a future-oriented endeavor. This can be difficult for at least three reasons. First, the normative developmental tendency for youth is to have limited future orientation. Second, most likely the defendant has not been adjudicated. Third, "You don't know what you don't know." It is difficult for youthful defendants to discuss engaging in services/programs that they don't know exist.

A helpful way to start this inquiry is to ask defendants to identify the areas in which they currently need help. From a developmental perspective, defendants may not be able to identify these areas because they may not appreciate the consequences of the behavior/activity. Therefore, the expert should be prepared to inquire about clinically relevant areas. For example, imagine that a 17-year-old male defendant has described extensive use of alcohol and marijuana. As a clinician you realize this is problematic for numerous reasons and have developed a hypothesis concerning what role substances play in his life. Yet, the defendant may not spontaneously identify the need for substance abuse treatment. The clinician can point out problems associated with drug and alcohol use and ask, "What would you do if you have the opportunity to participate in drug/alcohol treatment?" If the 17-year-old defendant says, "I don't need it," that is telling and potentially clinically relevant. So is the response, "Yeah, I would do it."

If the same defendant has a history of not engaging in services when offered, the clinician should ask the defendant to explain this. This inquiry could begin with "Help me understand why you would participate in treatment, when in the past treatment was offered but you didn't participate." This could lead to a discussion in which the defendant explains the role his peers and environment played in preventing participation in services and continued substance use.

Interviews with Caregivers

As described in Chapter 1 regarding the dependency factor, the *Miller* decision indicates that a matter to be considered is "[T]he family and home environment that surrounds him—from which he cannot usually extricate himself—no matter how brutal or dysfunctional." Thus, the scope for interviews with caregivers is broader than simply the defendant's development over time. It also includes how the defendant interacted with family as well as the strains and lifestyles of those with whom the defendant lived.

The explicit references to family (and implicitly to caregivers) is an important way *Miller* evaluations are distinct from evaluations typically conducted in adult court. Thus, caregivers have a unique role. While they could be considered third-party informants or collaterals, from a developmental perspective and for these evaluations, caregivers should be thought of as a vital source for obtaining developmental and background information. (If a report is written and the caregivers were not interviewed, the clinician should explain why.)

Many defendants have more than one main caregiver during their lives. Multiple people (e.g., grandmother, mother, and aunt) may have acted as caregivers over time. This should be considered when scheduling interviews with caregivers; it might influence who is interviewed as well as add context to the interviews themselves. For example, suppose you learn that a defendant moved back and forth between her maternal aunt's and her mother's residence for most of her life. You would probably want to interview both women in that case. You would also want to learn why the defendant transitioned from one residence to another, what the neighborhood was like in each residence, how the transition was explained to the defendant each time it occurred, and the emotional and behavioral impact on the defendant of the move.

The interview with the caregiver(s) should begin with a notification of the limits of confidentiality. The example of the notification given to the defendant can be adapted for this purpose. In many ways, interviewing the caregiver involves covering the same terrain as when interviewing the defendant. Although it is unlikely that the caregiver will provide useful information related to how the offense unfolded, the caregiver could provide valuable information about what was occurring in the family and neighborhood around the time of the offense. It is important to explain to interviewees that nothing that is revealed will be considered "off the record."

Other Collateral Interviews

The clinician should be aware of any professional parameters associated with interviewing collateral sources, including caregivers. For example, consistent with Specialty Guidelines (2013; section 6.04), provide a notification of limitations to the collateral at the start of the interview. The example of the notification provided to the defendant can be modified to suit interviews with collaterals and caregivers.

We noted earlier that in resentencing cases, it is sometimes helpful to interview prison officers who supervised or observed the inmate's work. Obtaining such an interview typically will require the help of the party requesting the evaluation, who in turn must typically consult with the prison's legal department before the collateral interview can occur.

Collateral interviews can generate data for any of the *Miller* factors. Clinicians are advised to think "outside the box" when generating potential sources for collateral interviews. Sources can include family members other than the caregivers, family acquaintances, peers, teachers, coaches, and religious leaders.

Peers sometimes can describe what was going on in the defendant's household prior to and around the time of offense, the defendant's relationship with the peer group, and the defendant's behavior and demeanor. The following exemplifies how a peer interview can provide information related to the dependency and offense contact factors. In an interview with Sharon, the defendant, she described running away from home to avoid being abused by her mother's boyfriend. Sharon said that while on the run she slept in the street or would spend days at the house of a friend, Kate. The clinician interviewed Kate and Kate's mother, Vickie, as she allowed the defendant to stay at her house. They described how Sharon's demeanor changed about six months after her mother's boyfriend began living in Sharon's house. Vickie stated that she let Sharon stay with them when she wanted because she was concerned that "he was doing something to her." Kate recalled what Sharon said her mother's boyfriend "did to her." Kate had promised Sharon she would not tell anyone because he threatened to hurt Sharon's mother if the police or authorities found out. Despite there being no official record of the abuse, the description Kate gave was very similar to what Sharon provided.

Collateral interviews can help fill in details about prior treatment attempts. The aunt of a 15-year-old defendant might report that he did not consistently attend therapy because his mother was not willing to spend what little money she had on public transportation for treatment she considered to be a waste of time and "for rich people." The aunt added that the defendant's mother told her he should go to boot camp or military school instead. This information is useful for many reasons. It corroborates what the defendant said, provides additional relevant information on why that treatment was a "failure," and provides topics to pursue in subsequent interviews.

As with any other source of interview data, clinicians should be cognizant of issues related to the response style of collateral interviewees. The issue of response style and inconsistencies across data sources were discussed earlier in this chapter. We encourage the clinician to bring significant inconsistencies to the attention of the person being interviewed. In a nonconfrontational manner, ask the interviewee to explain the inconsistencies.

Structured Assessment Methods

Structured assessment tools, such as measures of psychopathology and personality, will be most relevant for the decisional, dependency, and prospects for rehabilitation factors. Various psychological tests and assessment tools of potential relevance have been identified in Chapter 3. We recommend selecting measures based on the needs of each case. This section focuses on those considerations.

The Value of Multiple Data Sources

Consider the degree to which evidence for the various factors obtained through records and interviews needs corroboration by additional data obtained by methods less dependent on the errors associated with those sources. For example, if the records contain results of two previous cognitive tests but the results differ significantly, and if the defendant's cognitive ability is a relevant issue, then administering cognitive testing may be necessary, along with a closer examination of school records and performance on standardized academic testing. In contrast, if nothing in the records suggests that the defendant is cognitively impaired and, based on your interactions with the defendant, your clinical opinion is that the defendant's cognitive abilities are within the average range, you may not need to administer a test of cognitive abilities.

Normative Comparison

Consider the degree to which norms provided by tools will assist you in making norm-based comparisons between the defendant and others of similar and different age. This issue is particularly important when gathering data related to decisional immaturity and prospects for rehabilitation. Many psychological tests of personality, cognitive ability, and psychopathology have appropriate norms for comparing the defendant's needs and areas appropriate for intervention to reduce criminogenic factors. Being able to use norms to compare a defendant to other adolescents or adult inmates can be especially valuable in situations where the expert was asked for an opinion about the degree to which the defendant is the "rare" case with no prospects for rehabilitation.

Validity and Feasibility

Consider the evidence for validity of the measures, especially regarding validation with individuals of demographic, racial/ethnic, and legally contextual circumstances similar to those of the defendant. Certainly the administration of multiple tests may be challenging to the defendant's motivation and require substantial effort. Another factor related to feasibility is being cognizant of evidentiary standards discussed in Chapter 4.

Temporal Relevance in Resentencing Cases

In most resentencing cases, the prisoner has matured considerably since the time of the sentencing, which often occurred decades ago. Administering measures of decisional and dependency characteristics will be of little value in describing potentially mitigating factors retrospectively. More relevant will be measures of current capacities to provide data for prospects for rehabilitation.

Conclusion

The data-collection process described in this chapter is demanding in scope, complexity, diversity of data sources, and the time invested. This is related to two main features of *Miller* sentencing and resentencing evaluations. First, many facets of a defendant's life and personality are relevant for the *Miller* factors. Second, the consequences of these evaluations and the subsequent legal decisions in *Miller* cases are very significant. Both warrant intensive time and attention to detail in the data-collection process.

The value of good data collection will be apparent as one moves to the next step: the interpretation of the data to form opinions about the defendant relevant for the *Miller* factors. The two phases are related in important ways; clinicians must be entertaining possible interpretations while they are collecting the data and seek data that are relevant to alternative or conflicting interpretations. Chapter 6 addresses the interpretation process.

Interpretation 6

This chapter begins with a brief discussion of general principles regarding examiners' interpretations of the data collected according to the process described in Chapter 5. It is followed by guidance for interpretations associated with each of *Miller*'s psycholegal factors.

General Considerations

Shaping one's interpretations in *Miller* cases requires attending to several principles that apply to most forensic evaluations. These include understanding the forensic clinician's role in legal cases, types of inferences, and how inferences are formed.

Role Clarity Regarding Expert Opinions

The clinician's role is to describe aspects of the defendant's development, behavior, and life circumstances that are relevant to the court's decisions about mitigation in sentencing based on immaturity. This means providing the court with clinical and empirical data that, in the opinion of the expert, are reliably related to each *Miller* factor. For example, the clinician will attempt to form an opinion about whether and how certain factors of immaturity influenced (or did not influence) the defendant's role and participation in the offense. These are the types of questions the clinician seeks to answer while engaging in the interpretation process.

The court will then consider those opinions and the reasoning that underlies these opinions when addressing the legal questions that the court must answer. Among those legal questions are the youth's culpability (blameworthiness) and whether the youth meets certain legal requirements for a specific sentence. Clinicians should not express opinions about those ultimately legal question—what sentence should be imposed.

The Relation of Data to Opinions

Data are facts the clinician uses to make inferences that form expert opinions. A youth's high score compared to peer norms on a psychometric measure of impulsiveness is a fact (data). Yet, the clinician's eventual expert opinion that the youth "is more impulsive than her age peers" is an inference or interpretation. This is because that opinion requires the expert's judgment as to whether the score is valid and whether other data in the case confirm or are inconsistent with what the score suggests. The clinician should be prepared to explain how the opinion was formed in that broader sense, not merely based on a score.

Similarly, causal opinions—e.g., "his involvement in the offense was due to peer influence"—require careful consideration regarding the process of arriving at them. If peers were involved and exerted pressure, that is a possible explanation for the youth's involvement. But, like the test score in the previous example, that fact does not necessarily mean that peer pressure was the primary motivator for the youth. That will require the clinician's consideration of the youth's susceptibility to such pressure and various details of the offense to arrive at an opinion about the role of peer pressure in the case.

Often the "links" between facts and inferential opinion will require close attention to formal psychiatric diagnostic criteria or the use of relevant research and theory. For example, the fact that a youth has had multiple traumatizing experiences (potentially relevant for the dependency factor) is not sufficient alone to offer an opinion about a trauma-related disorder, such as Post-Traumatic Stress Disorder (for which exposure to traumatic events is only one of seven required conditions). Similarly, factual evidence regarding a youth's abilities related to decision making must be considered in the context of developmental research and theory (see Chapter 3) when making inferences related to the decisional factor.

Corroborating Information

Data obtained from only one source are always at risk of source-related error. Inferences are best supported by observations when there is more than one corroborating source. This applies to data from different methods (e.g., psychological testing, interviews, records), as well as data from different sources within those methods (e.g., multiple tests, multiple interviewees, across records). This will be possible if the examiner has used several methods and sources as described in Chapter 5 and has used the data-collection process dynamically—that is, using data as they arise to identify additional data sources of potential relevance.

Alternative Hypotheses and Interpretations

Initial opinions quite often are open to alternative interpretations. One should strive to imagine those alternatives and determine whether the data better fit the original interpretation. During this process, experienced forensic mental health examiners try, in effect, to prove themselves wrong. The benefits of this practice are substantial, helping to identify bias that might have shaped the original hypothesis, due to insufficient data, bias, faulty logic, or advocacy (Kassin et al., 2013; Neal & Grisso, 2014; Zapf et al., 2018). Depending on the outcome of this process, the clinician may have varying levels of confidence in the final opinion. Finally, the process reduces the likelihood that the clinician will be caught off guard in oral testimony by alternative hypotheses offered by attorneys in cross-examination.

Preparation for Addressing the *Miller* Factors

We recommend that before making interpretations to address the *Miller* factors, the clinician should draft a general history and developmental foundation regarding the defendant and the family. This will not necessarily appear in the clinician's report, but organizing a formulation, holistic picture, or general profile of the family, the defendant, and the defendant's history can aid the interpretive process.

Constructing this family and defendant formulation is not essentially forensic, being closer to what one does in general developmental and clinical assessments. Included in this working picture of the case are various developmental characteristics, education and clinical (mental health) status and history, personality, and history of illegal activity. It should include relevant family dynamics, as well as special emphasis on various aspects of maturity and immaturity regarding intellectual and cognitive abilities and psychosocial maturity. This provides a context within which later *Miller*-related inferences will be made.

Given this preparation, let us consider issues that frequently arise in the interpretive process for each of the *Miller* factors. Subsequent sections also address special considerations in *Miller* resentencing cases and interpretations associated with irreparable corruption.

Inferences Related to the Decisional Maturity Factor

One of the major objectives in addressing the decisional factor is to arrive at inferences about differences, around the time of the offense, between the defendant and other adolescents or adults in decisional maturity (that is, regarding risk taking, impulsiveness, and decisional judgment). One does this by using relevant data and the formulation described earlier in this chapter. In addition, the evaluator should determine whether the data can address the potential effects of contextual factors on the individual's decision making. As noted in Chapter 3, most youth can respond more effectively in controlled, structured situations and less effectively when confronted with emotionally stressful situations. Can the data identify whether this is any more so or less so for this particular defendant?

When making inferences about decisional characteristics at the time of the offense, one must be cautious about making inferences based on the current performance of the defendant during interviews and testing. In *Miller* resentencing cases, the time between the current evaluation and the offense may be decades, so that current performance is unlikely to represent the defendant's status at the time of the offense. In *Miller* sentencing cases, the time differences are shorter but still often a year or two. In those cases, whether current performance can be inferred to approximate status at the time of the offense will require comparing it to other sources of data—for example, prior psychological or educational testing closer in time to the offense.

Even without prior testing, however, one often can compare current status to evidence of past status identified in school or mental health records, and interview data from family and others regarding the defendant's status at that earlier time. For example, imagine a case in which multiple interview sources indicate that around the time of the offense, teachers (data source A) report that the defendant's abilities were not as developed as most of the students. Current testing of decisional abilities (data source B) indicates that the defendant has relevant impairments compared to others his current age. Then the clinician reviews any data (data source C) bearing on whether events in the time between the offense and the present might have reasonably improved (or delayed) the youth's development of decisional abilities. Thus, in the absence of prior testing, data from sources A + B + C may allow the clinician to make a reasonable inference about the defendant's decision-making capacity around the time of the offense.

Inferences Related to the Dependency Factor

As described in Chapter 2, the dependency factor includes consideration of several things: degree of autonomy and dependency (as a social condition and as personal capacities); family and environmental circumstances of disadvantage, abuse, or trauma; and factors outside the youth's control that impacted development. We suggest focusing the interpretive process on two primary questions. First, is there evidence from which to infer that the juvenile experienced social circumstances that placed developmental burdens on the youth, especially circumstances that youths typically have limited power or means to avoid? Second, is there evidence to infer that this youth's capacities for adaptive autonomy in dealing with these burdens were relatively less or more than other juveniles? The following hypothetical case illustrates an inferential process for addressing these two questions.

Pat, now age 18, is facing sentencing for a murder he committed at age 16. The shooting was gang-related. Pat is the oldest of three siblings and was raised in a two-parent household in a neighborhood marred by poverty and a high level of gang violence. These are not conditions from which Pat would have been able to extricate himself.

Inferences about how these factors may have played a role in Pat's dependency should be based on the data collected, then interpreted in light of research and theory. Pat claimed, and police documents affirmed, that nearly all the males in his immediate and extended family were gang-involved and that he did not join the gang until he was 15, which was considered "old." He described how his previous efforts to avoid joining the gang resulted in his being injured, which his mother and medical records confirm. The data obtained from Pat and written records are consistent with empirically and theoretically recognized factors (e.g., community and family) that contribute to youth gang membership (Gilman et al., 2014; Taylor & Smith, 2013).

The second question addresses this youth's capacities to operate autonomously relative to other youths. Pat told the clinician he joined a gang two months after his father died. The clinician inferred that Pat was particularly vulnerable to the influence of the gang when he joined because he was still grieving and displayed signs of depression and decreased functioning. These inferences can be supported by various facts. After his father died, school records show his truancy increased and school performance declined. According to his mother, he started ignoring curfew two or three times a week. His only other involvement with the criminal justice system occurred six months later (a misdemeanor, which was dismissed). According to current testing data, he scores higher in depressive symptoms and family discord than most other youth and higher than 75% of adjudicated youth.

Inferences Relating Developmental Factors to the Offense Context

Miller cases ask for opinions about the relevance of the individual's status on the decisional and dependency factors when applied to the offense for which the person has been convicted. As discussed in Chapter 2, this inferential process is similar to the one employed by forensic clinicians in insanity cases, when they examine the potential role of defendants' mental illnesses in their offenses.

Doing so requires reviewing the offense in detail using various sources of data, including the defendant, police and court records, and collateral sources. Next, the clinician forms opinions concerning the role, if any, that the defendant's mental condition played at various points in the unfolding of the offense. In *Miller* cases, however, inferences about the individual's decisional and dependency characteristics—as well as mental disorder—constitute the salient individual characteristics that drive the analysis. The following case illustrates this process.

John, age 46, was evaluated in a *Miller* resentencing case. Records indicated, and John acknowledged, that at age 15 he shot at a parked van from behind it. The bullets entered the van through the small back windows and killed the two rear passengers. Those in the front seat were not harmed. During the interview, he described how he eagerly volunteered to "shoot at the van" because his friends teased him about being a "runt" and not a "man." He thought this would improve the way his peers viewed him. He explained that, at the time, he did not consider the possibility of killing anyone. He shot at the back of the van because he didn't think anyone was sitting there. His description of his motivation at the time he committed the crime reflects normative developmental immaturity related to peer influence and peer pressure.

John's words alone, however, were not enough to make this inference, nor did they address whether he was different from other youth in his susceptibility to peer influence. Additional data provided some collaborative information. Letters that John's friends wrote to him between the time of the offense and his adjudication echoed the assertion that his friends' intentions were for John to "scare them, not kill anyone." In a collateral interview, Mark, a member of this peer group, recounted that John was frequently teased and called "Mickey Mouse," that he was more often the target of such teasing than the others in the group, and consequently he often tried to act tough. Finally, John's parents still had a folder with old school records, indicating that school counselors suspected that John had Attention-Deficit/Hyperactivity Disorder. They also noted several instances in which he reacted impulsively when pressured in social situations involving peers in the classroom and during recess.

Inferences About Prospects for Rehabilitation

Prospects for rehabilitation is a fundamental *Miller* factor requiring inferences about the defendant's potential for change through therapeutic, educational, and skill-building interventions as well as further maturation. Almost all the research topics described in Chapter 3, as well as a wide range of data, are potentially relevant for shaping prospects for rehabilitation inferences. Chapter 2 offers some conceptual guidance for using those data to arrive at prospects for rehabilitation opinions.

Framing the Questions

When forming prospects for rehabilitation opinions, there are two ways to frame the question one is trying to answer: (a) as a prediction that a person will or will not be rehabilitated and (b) as a relative estimate of the likelihood of rehabilitation. The second way of framing the question is the appropriate one, for the following reasons.

The difference between a yes/no prediction of an outcome and an estimate of its likelihood is well known within a different forensic assessment context—risk of reoffending. In that area, for a very long time we have understood why we should not try to predict that a person will or won't engage in a future violent behavior. Ample research has taught us that dichotomous predictions of this kind are fraught with false-positive error, so much so that we are more often wrong than right when we make them (Monahan, 1982). We have learned instead to estimate the relative likelihood of recidivism (e.g., low, moderate, or high relative to others), which research tells us has more potential for validity.

Similarly, the proper question for prospects for rehabilitation opinions is not "Will this person be rehabilitated?" but "What is the relative potential for rehabilitation?" One hopes to provide the court with all the evidence that weighs for and against rehabilitation, but not to predict an outcome. Thus, the clinician is aiming for opinions about the low, moderate, or high likelihood of rehabilitation compared to other defendants, based on the individual's amenability and various possible rehabilitative interventions and situational factors. The ability to provide an accurate estimate (low, moderate, or high) of successful rehabilitation will decrease in accuracy as the length of time of the prediction increases.

Making Prospective Inferences Based on Retrospective Inferences

When engaging in the prospects for rehabilitation analysis, one will be making retrospective inferences as well as prospective ones. Retrospective analysis involves using information about past rehabilitation efforts as data for inferences about prospective potential, when combined with one's current assessment of the defendant's needs.

While doing this, it is important to employ the person–environment perspective as described in Chapter 2. One is considering data related to the person's amenability (person characteristics) as well as data related to the types of interventions that may be applied. When engaged in a retrospective analysis of the success or failure of past rehabilitation efforts, identify what the youth was like then and what needed to change (the amenability component), as well as whether the program was matched to those needs and was of a reasonable evidence-based quality and duration. Consider also the possibility that the intervention might have had effects that were criminogenic—that is, contributed to further offending. For example, in reviewing John's records you learn, three years ago, when John was 13 years old, he was enrolled in and successfully completed a juvenile justice work readiness program. The probation officer's notes indicate this program was chosen to provide

John with structure and adult supervision. During your interview with John he beamed as he described how the program taught him what to wear to a job interview and how he participated in mock interviews. John went on to explain that the other participants were at least three years his senior and often each day after the program session a few would let him “hang with them.” They convinced him since he was the youngest, he should do some illegal things (stealing, breaking and entering) for the group because, if he was caught, the police would go easy on someone so young.

The person–environment, interactive approach should also be used prospectively, identifying the defendant’s existing needs and criminogenic factors and describing what services are needed to address them. It is difficult to know what services will be available over the course of a lengthy incarceration. Consequently, clinicians should think of the theoretical environment or services and not limit themselves to what currently exists.

Miller Resentencing and Rehabilitation Inferences

Miller resentencing cases will require a similar logic, although the retrospective analysis will focus especially on the individual’s characteristics and needs while the person has been in the adult correctional system, together with the services that were provided to address these needs. As discussed in Chapter 5, in our experience, most of the needs of the individual will not have been addressed. If this is the case, consider the individual’s behavior over the course of the incarceration, such as voluntary participation in activities such as work, education, or group activities; disciplinary actions; and documented prosocial acts. These data will assist in making inferences about the prisoner’s maturity trajectory while incarcerated and how that relates to potential for rehabilitation.

Inferences Related to Irreparable Corruption

The court and retaining parties will expect information that will allow them to address the two elements of irreparable corruption: that is, whether the defendant (a) will be a lifetime offender and (b) will never respond to rehabilitation efforts.

We have described in Chapters 2 and 3 why clinicians have no way to offer a valid prediction that a defendant is a lifetime-persistent offender who can never be rehabilitated. Moreover, as discussed in the previous section on prospects for rehabilitation, such yes/no predictions about future behavior typically are fraught with false-positive error because they address outcomes with a very low base rate (rare).

Using the model offered by Fairfax-Columbo et al. (2019) (see Chapter 2) does not allow one to overcome those barriers to forming a valid opinion that a person is a lifetime violent persister who can never change. However, the content of their three-step model describes very well the information and opinions clinicians can offer to assist the court in its weighing of the issue. First, clinicians can describe why the "default," based on research, is that the youth can be rehabilitated. Second. they can seek to form opinions that this defendant's characteristics more closely fit patterns (in research) for those who more often desist in offending in late adolescence or are more similar to those who persist beyond adolescence (although this does not mean they will be lifetime persisters). And third, as described in the previous section on prospects for rehabilitation, clinicians can form opinions about factors that suggest a lower, moderate, or higher degree of potential for change, even if they cannot validly predict that change is impossible.

Conclusion

Our guidance for making inferences to reach opinions for *Miller* sentencing and resentencing cases has been far from formulaic. This is not peculiar to *Miller* cases; formulas for interpretation are few in most clinical and forensic assessment processes. Specific facts vary greatly across cases, so the process must be guided primarily by the types of general principles that we reviewed in the first section of this chapter. The quality of one's interpretations will depend especially on (a) a clear view of the questions one is addressing (and those that are not relevant); (b) the application of empirical research in the field to guide one's use of the data to address those questions; (c) the generation of alternative hypotheses; and (d) one's search for confirming and disconfirming data applied to each of the hypotheses. The inferences and opinions having been determined, the final step is their communication to the court in a manner that allows them to be clearly understood. Those communications—a written report and testimony—are the focus of the final chapter.

7 Report Writing and Testimony

Reports and testimony describe, in a clear and accessible fashion, the evaluation's methodology, relevant data, and expert opinions related to the legal issues at hand. Excellent general guidance on forensic report writing and testimony is provided in other resources (e.g., Brodsky & Gutheil, 2016; DeMier & Otto, 2017; Karson & Nadkarni, 2013; Otto et al., 2014). Therefore, we focus on aspects of communication that are particularly germane to *Miller* sentencing and resentencing evaluations, as well as evaluations for cases in which youth face *de facto* life sentences.

We begin with an overview of certain particular challenges associated with conveying the results of *Miller* evaluations. We then offer advice for communicating with attorneys during the report-writing process, followed by a suggested template for *Miller* reports. Finally, recommendations for oral testimony are offered, first for depositions and then for courtroom testimony.

Special Demands of *Miller* Reports and Testimony

Many judges and attorneys involved with *Miller* cases will have more experience with adult criminal cases than juvenile cases. They might not be familiar with the developmental and clinical characteristics of adolescents that provide the foundation for the expert's opinions regarding the *Miller* factors. Moreover, because *Miller* sentencing and resentencing cases are relatively new, there are limited precedents for how to prepare and present the evaluations.

Describing Developmental Foundations

The expert's interpretations and opinions, in reports and during testimony, should be grounded in research and knowledge of developmental psychology. When communicating with the court, it is critical to explain concepts in a way that non-clinicians can understand, especially if they have limited experience with juvenile cases. As discussed in Chapters 2 and 3, less familiar topics might include brain development neuroscience and its relevance for the *Miller* factors, research on the malleability of youth, and certain important clinical conditions (such as trauma or depression) in the context of adolescent development. Most reports do not require detailed discussions of these topics. However, be prepared to present them in an accessible way during oral testimony.

Defining the *Miller* Psycholegal Factors

The psycholegal factors presented in this book are a translation of the *Miller* factors (legal language) into parallel concepts that are meaningful to a forensic clinician. However, for reports and testimony, experts should speak the language of the court whenever possible. This is consistent with the field's emphasis on a key aspect of competency: understanding the legal context in which one works (Specialty Guidelines for Forensic Psychology, 2013, Guideline 2.04). Therefore, we recommend that clinicians "back-translate" the psycholegal concepts to those provided in law. This is reflected in the report template in the Appendix.

Limited Precedent for *Miller* Evaluations

Because of the relative recency of the *Miller* decision, neither the legal field nor the forensic mental health discipline has a widely recognized standard approach to conducting *Miller* evaluations or presenting the findings in written form. This is apparently the first book to describe how to conduct these evaluations and convey the findings to the retaining party. Even the courts and attorneys often lack a clear notion of what is required of experts in these cases. This places an extra burden on experts to be explicit and transparent about their evaluation procedures, definitions of relevant concepts, and logic for arriving at interpretations.

Report Writing: Communication with Referral Source

As indicated in Chapter 4, we urge clinicians to have a detailed conversation with the retaining party regarding the individualized nature of the potential case before accepting it. What happens after the clinician conducts the evaluation and develops clinical opinions differs by type of referral source. When conducting a court-ordered *Miller* evaluation, the expert will have little communication with the court until the report is written and tendered to the defense counsel, prosecutor, and judge. However, when the evaluation is not court-ordered, the expert often communicates with the retaining party about the clinical opinions prior to writing the report, for the following reasons.

For evaluations that are not court ordered, we recommend that examiners share their clinical opinions with the retaining party before writing the report. Be prepared to explain how the opinions were reached. It has been our experience that some of the data and/or their significance will be new to the attorney. Discussing the results before writing a report allows the retaining party to decide how to proceed with the expert. If the opinion does not support the attorney's objectives or strategies, the attorney may instruct the clinician not to write a report. In those situations, clinicians may be required to return records supplied by the retaining party; provide the retaining party copies of some or all of the data the clinician generated and relied upon; and/or safely store documents until they can be destroyed. Local laws and the written agreement between the clinician and retaining party should dictate the handling of such records at this stage. (See Specialty Guidelines for Forensic Psychology, 2013, section 10.8, for further guidance.) If a report is requested, establish a timeline for when it is due.

Recommended Template for a *Miller* Report

Others have provided guidance on writing forensic reports in general (DeMier & Otto, 2017; Grisso, 2010; Karson, 2015; Karson & Nadkarni, 2013; Zwartz, 2018), on writing reports for juvenile evaluations (e.g., (Salekin, 2015), and on writing reports for sentencing evaluations (see Melton et al, 2018). Here we describe key sections of a report template we recommend for *Miller* sentencing, resentencing, or *de facto* life cases. The Appendix contains a template that should be modified to incorporate and reference relevant local legal cases.

Some aspects of the report unique or tailored to the particular legal issue can necessitate long sections. Clinical judgment and audience awareness should drive decisions about organization. Legal scholars suggest that legal audiences expect documents with headings and subheadings (Schiess, 2014). As part of their training, lawyers are instructed to provide the court with a persuasive story that has many chapters. Frequently, the information within the chapter is not presented sequentially. Instead, it is presented by topic, which equates to subheadings or landmarks for the reader. Consistent with this, think of each section of the report as a chapter and use subheadings to organize the longer sections.

Reason for Evaluation

Explain the reason the evaluation was requested, who requested it, and what was requested. Identify the offense charged (or the charge of which the defendant was convicted) without describing the underlying facts. For example: "On December 03, 20XX, a jury found Mr. Defendant guilty of first-degree murder. He is awaiting a sentencing hearing."

The next sentences depends on the particulars of the jurisdiction as well as the nature of the case (sentencing or resentencing). If the jurisdiction has case law or controlling statute: "Consistent with (cite statute or controlling case in present jurisdiction), which implements the holding of U.S. Supreme Court in *Miller v. Alabama* (use if a sentencing case)/*Montgomery v. Louisiana* (use if a resentencing case)." If the jurisdiction does not have case law or controlling statute: "Consistent with the holding of U.S. Supreme Court in *Miller v. Alabama* (use if a sentencing case)/ *Montgomery v. Louisiana* (use if a resentencing case)."

Clinically Relevant Language from *Miller*

The template in the Appendix includes a description of the *Miller* factors pertinent to most cases. As needed, the relevant legal language and content should be altered to be consistent with relevant law in the jurisdiction. This is particularly important when the defendant is facing a *de facto* life sentence. The risk of incompetency factor described in Chapter 1 is not included, as we believe it will be used very infrequently.

Sources of Data and Evaluation Techniques

As in most forensic reports, this section should list all sources of data reviewed and requested. This should include (a) a list of all interviews (with defendant and collateral informants), including location, dates, and length of time for each interview, (b) a list of all tests/instruments given to the defendant, including date given, and (c) any unsuccessful attempts to collect data. Normally this section would also include a list of all documents reviewed, including the dates of the documents. Because *Miller* cases often involve copious amounts of records, we suggest providing this list as an appendix to the report. Finally, in this section explain how informed consent was obtained.

Account of the Offense Based on Police and Court Records

In this section, provide an official account of the offense. We recognize that if the evaluation is conducted before the defendant is convicted, there may be different official accounts. Consider using the indictment document, police documents, or some document that describes the allegations and the charges that were used to process the case. While this may not reflect the charges of which the defendant will ultimately be convicted, our suggestion is consistent with what the clinician does in a not guilty by reason of insanity or death penalty evaluation. If the defendant has been convicted, we suggest relying on the transcript where the fact finder announced the guilty finding and charges and may have described the underlying act(s). Supplement with police documents describing the underlying allegations, as needed.

Review of Relevant Records

Records for these evaluations are often voluminous and can include the defendant's records as well as those of family members. Keep two things in mind when presenting a written review of the records. One, present a concise description of the records you relied upon in forming your clinical opinion(s). This review should let the reader know exactly what in the record you found relevant and significant and, consistent with rules of discovery, include enough information to allow the judge and attorneys to locate the portion being cited. Two, use subheadings and, when necessary, sub-subheadings. For example, a subheading might be "Records Related to Ms. Frame, the Defendant's Mother," and under that might be the sub-subheadings "Mental Health Treatment Records" and "Court and Police Records." Typical subheadings will reference records related to school, mental health, and prior court involvement, but they might also include documents from social services, hospitals, and others depending on particulars of the case.

Although the use of footnotes in legal writings has been debated (Magat, 2010), consider using them because they allow readers to find the documents for themselves as needed without disrupting their flow while reading. Such specificity could also prove useful to a higher court.

Mental Status and Behavioral Observations

This section describes the defendant's mental status, presentation, and demeanor during the evaluation process. It could also be used to describe relevant characteristics of any interviewees that may have impacted their response style and/or clinical observations that are relevant to the *Miller* factors. For example, imagine conducting a resentencing evaluation in which the defendant's only living parent had two strokes, impacting his memory and speech. Although the strokes occurred after the defendant was incarcerated, how they impacted the father's ability to participate in the interview could be a noteworthy observation.

As another example, imagine interviewing Ms. Thomas, the mother of a defendant convicted of murder at 15 years of age. During the interview, Ms. Thomas nodded off multiple times. The evaluator asked her about this behavior, and, after some discussion, Ms. Thomas revealed that she had taken an illicit drug prior to the interview. Both the behavior and her explanation for it should be noted in this section.

Finally, the nature of the data collected should determine where to place this section and how much detail to provide. If, as in the case with the examples above, the behavior or observations could help the reader understand the manner in which an interviewee presented and responded to questions, then put this section before the relevant interview sections.

Relevant Information Obtained from Interviewees

This section presents information about the defendant and family up until the offense for which the defendant will be sentenced occurred. Begin with a statement about the consistency of reports across interviewees and describe how relevant inconsistencies will be handled. For example, "As historians, Mr. Jackson and his parents were fairly consistent with each other. The source of any relevant inconsistencies will be noted."

Subheadings are particularly useful in this section. For example, one section heading might be "X's Background" (where X is the name of the parent or guardian). Use clinical discretion to determine the appropriate subsections. Consider a single-parent household where the father worked three low-wage jobs and was rarely home. When home, he drank excessively. This could provide data related to the father's behavior when intoxicated and the level of supervision the defendant received and shed a better light on the defendant's own substance use. After brief contextual remarks, the father's section might have two subheadings: "Job History" and "Substance Use History." In contrast, factors such as the father's level of education or lack of trauma history are less relevant. Although these types of data may have been explored in the interview process, they do not warrant inclusion in the report. Finally, as in most forensic cases, this section will also contain relevant background or historical information related to the defendant.

Defendant's Account of the Offense

This section provides the court with the defendant's account of the offense as it occurred. It should include data related to the defendant's current understandings of the defendant's role in the offense and the offense's impact on others. In this section, use direct quotes of what the defendant recalled and reported to the expert rather than paraphrasing the information provided.

Clinical Opinion Regarding *Miller* Factors

In this section, provide clinical opinions for each *Miller* factor, as well as for the two questions in irreparable corruption if applicable, as well as a complete account of how you arrived at them. This will include examples of the data and the research, theory, and clinical logic used to arrive at the opinion. The clinician should also explain why alternative hypotheses were considered and rejected and what variables might impact one's confidence in the opinion. For example, imagine conducting an evaluation in which the defendant is the only remaining living member of his immediate family. One would have more confidence in the data he provided if it can be corroborated in other ways. If documents related to prior interactions with the legal or social justice system are no longer available, you might be less confident, and that should be noted in the report.

Additional Considerations for *Miller* Resentencing Reports

Because of its retrospective nature, the report format for *Miller* resentencing evaluations differs in three significant ways. First, in the "Identifying Information" section, it is important to indicate how long the defendant has been incarcerated for the instant offense. This provides a time frame in which to anchor issues of maturity and potential for rehabilitation.

The second difference is that the "Review of Relevant Records" section includes the defendant's prison file. As many defendants have large prison files, it can be helpful to organize them by categories such as "Disciplinary Reports," "Medical/Mental Health," and "Education and Programing." As is the case with any forensic report, the subsections should be tailored to fit the particulars of the case. Depending on the number and pattern of disciplinary reports, it may be helpful to use a chart to present the information with column headings for date of report, age, description, type (major/minor), and outcome. In addition to being concise, this presentation allows the reader to quickly discern potentially significant patterns or changes in the nature and frequency of the reports. For example, for a defendant who repeatedly received mental health services and/or psychotropic medication, it might be helpful to create a chart that overlays these services with disciplinary reports. The charts used in the written report may be useful during testimony if blow-ups are made and shown to the court as testimony proceeds.

The third additional component of a *Miller* resentencing report is a "Defendant's Account of Life in Prison" section. Consider organizing these data with the same subsections used to present the defendant's prison file.

Depositions

Because *Miller* cases involve serious crimes and long sentences, *Miller* examiners may be asked by their retaining attorney, in some jurisdictions, to participate in a deposition at the request of opposing counsel. An expert witness deposition is a legal proceeding in which the opposing counsel is provided the opportunity of discovery. The purpose of discovery is to allow opposing counsel to ask questions to learn what expert evidence the other party will bring to trial, so that opposing counsel will have ample and fair opportunity to prepare to challenge the expert in court. The attorney who has retained the expert will likely be at the deposition as well. A transcript will be made and can be used to challenge the expert during later court appearances if the expert's testimony is inconsistent with the deposition responses. In other words, the clinician should consider testimony provided during deposition no differently than testimony in court. Reviewing the deposition is useful to identify and inform the retaining party of any errors, and to prepare for expert testimony.

There are few rules for the deposing attorneys regarding the types of questions they can ask, as long as they pertain to the expert's testimony. The role of retaining counsel is to monitor the process and to object to any specific questions "for the record." From a clinician's perspective, the deposition offers an opportunity to see the opposing counsel in action. Deposition questions might reveal counsel's perceptions of problems or weaknesses in the clinician's methods, opinions, and report, suggesting possible points that counsel might raise in courtroom cross-examination. Because the deposition is a form of testimony, much of the following section is also applicable.

Testimony

The demands of testimony in *Miller* cases are not unlike those in capital sentencing cases. In this section, we focus on special issues related to testifying in *Miller* sentencing and resentencing evaluations.

Preparation for Testimony

Preparing to testify involves a combination of working independently and with the legal team. Before meeting with the attorneys, at a minimum, review the documents that were referenced in the report. Also review the report for errors and identify data-collection procedures that, in hindsight, you would like to have done differently.

The most important task at this stage is to begin internalizing the report. This means being able to explain what you were asked to do and what you did and describing relevant data and clinical opinions. You should be able to speak to these issues without frequently consulting the written report. Internalizing the report increases the productivity of meetings with the attorney, as the clinician will be better prepared to do a dry run or "mock" of the testimony. The internalization process will vary among experts and with regard to the specifics of the case at hand. For example, one of the authors of this book dictates a condensed version of the report onto her mobile phone and listens to that version repeatedly during the week before the attorney meeting.

Preparation time with the attorney might require more than one meeting. During this process, the examiner should not make any changes in the facts, interpretations, and opinions to which the examiner is already committed in the report. Depending on the attorney's style, the amount of time spent preparing together will vary, but at a minimum should include attention to the following:

- logistical information, such as the location of the courtroom, probable time to arrive for testimony, what the clinician can bring into the courtroom, and whether the clinician is allowed to be in the courtroom at any time other than when testifying
- aspects of the clinician's experience or curriculum vitae that should be highlighted in *voir dire*
- a dry run of the direct testimony, with the attorney asking the questions in the sequence expected during direct examination
- potential weaknesses in the evaluation process and the clinician's explanations for them
- possible issues the opposing counsel may raise on cross-examination, with the clinician offering potential answers to those questions
- a review of the opposing expert's report, if available.

The dry run or mock testimony is critical for several reasons, but three of them bear special attention: (a) answering the ultimate legal question, (b) testifying to matters for which one's methods do not allow for reliable opinions, and (c) dealing with nuances of language to avoid confusion during testimony.

First, the attorney needs to know how the clinician will respond if either side poses questions about the ultimate legal question. For example, in *Miller* cases, examiners might be asked their opinion as to whether the youth is "irreparably corrupt" or was "too immature at the time of the offense to warrant the maximum allowable sentence." As indicated in Chapter 4, although this is permissible in light of the Federal Rules of Evidence, many forensic scholars and clinicians believe the ultimate legal issue is beyond the purview of a clinician. Regardless of where you stand on this issue, it is important that you take the same position in writing and during testimony.

Second, the attorney might intend to ask questions that are beyond the clinician's ability to answer reliably because of scientific or data-based limits for their foundation. For example, the attorney might wish to ask the clinician's opinion about elements of irreparable corruption: "In your opinion, will James be a lifetime offender?" or "Is James incapable of rehabilitation?" We explained in Chapters 2 and 6 that current methods do not provide a reliable basis for answering "yes" or "no" to these prediction questions. Thus, the clinician might respond: "If asked that question, I will have to say that methods currently available to experts do not allow for reliable opinions on those matters. But if asked whether I have relevant information the court might consider, I do. This includes . . ." What needs to be conveyed to the attorney is the difference between (a) an opinion that a defendant "will" or "can never" be rehabilitated (which exceeds the clinician's ability to predict) and (b) an opinion regarding the defendant's prospects for rehabilitation by using reliable data that weigh more or less favorably regarding the defendant's rehabilitative change.

Finally, because legal and forensic mental health professions speak different languages, it is important to work on the wording of the attorney's questions to ensure they will elicit the intended response. Imagine that during the mock questioning, the attorney asks: "Doctor, do you believe the youth was more immature than his peers at the time of the offense?" The clinician should anticipate having difficulty answering the question because the youth was immature in some ways and not in others. The clinician might say: "If you word the question that way, I might simply respond 'Yes and no.' But if you ask: 'Are there any ways in which the youth was more immature . . .' here is how I would respond. Which response do you wish to have on record?"

As noted earlier, the dry run should also include questions that might be asked during cross-examination. Indeed, sometimes a defense attorney may want to ask those questions on direct examination, even if they create difficulty for the defense, in order to gain strategic control from a legal argumentative perspective.

After meeting with the attorney, the clinician should continue to prepare for testimony by incorporating any new information or decisions made during the discussions while further internalizing the report.

Responding to Questions Under Oath

The American Bar Association has provided some guidance for a witness to follow when being deposed (Epstein, 2014). We urge clinicians to also consider these rules when testifying in court. The first three are especially important when providing direct testimony and all apply when providing testimony under cross-examination:

1. Listen to the question.
2. Understand the question.
3. Think before you answer.
4. Provide the shortest and clearest answers possible.

During testimony, the clinician will most likely be asked: "Doctor, have you formed an opinion to a reasonable degree of psychological (or psychiatric) certainty?" Lawyers and forensic clinicians debate what this term "reasonable degree of psychological (or psychiatric) certainty" means (see Drogin et al., 2012). However, for forensic mental health experts, the practical explanation of this concept rests in the varied methodology used in the assessment, the consistency within and between the sources of data relied on, and the relevance and predictive power of the data.

Anticipating Cross-Examination in *Miller* Cases

Experts are more frequently called by the defense attorney than by prosecutors, but this is not always the case. This section describes potential arguments and responses to anticipate during questioning by either side. We focus on questions that require more than yes/no answers typically provided in cross-examination.

CROSS-EXAMINATION BY PROSECUTOR

The crimes in *Miller* and *Montgomery* were brutal. Many prosecutors will focus on the heinous or brutal nature of the present offense. Be prepared for a line of questioning that equates the nature of the offense with irreparable corruption and/or an indication that rehabilitation is not possible. In responding to this line of questioning, we urge clinicians to keep three points in mind. One, explain that you considered the defendant's role in the offense and have formed your opinion on that basis, not merely on the brutality of the offense. Two, as discussed in Chapters 2 and 3, explain that as a profession we cannot accurately predict the behaviors associated with irreparable corruption, especially among youth. Be prepared to reiterate the factors that you identified related to irreparable corruption as they apply to the case at hand. Three, explain how, in appraising the possibility of rehabilitation, you used an interactive person–environment framework to analyze the potential for rehabilitation. In doing so, past behavior alone is not the only thing considered.

The prosecutor may also pose questions aimed at demonstrating that the offense was planned or intentional and therefore was neither impulsive nor related to any of the "hallmarks" of youthful immaturity. In answer to this line of questioning, recognize that it is your task to place the defendant and the defendant's role in the offense in a developmentally appropriate context. Explain how you looked beyond "impulsiveness" to examine whether the "plan" suggested sophistication or naivete regarding anticipation of potential consequences. In the latter case, did the "plan" reflect immaturity associated with the broad range of indicators identified by the decisional and dependency factors (e.g., adolescent risk taking, peer influence, and lack of long-range time perspective, as identified in psychological literature)? Do not assume "maturity" simply because there was a "plan," but rather engage your forensic developmental expertise in analyzing the case. In addition, an individual's maturity is evidenced by much more than a single act. Broader reference to maturity and criminal sophistication can be provided, based on evidence developed throughout this evaluation.

Whether on direct or on cross-examination, prosecutors may pose questions highlighting the defendant's history of adverse life experiences, either in their absence or their presence. The prosecution could assert: "This defendant's background was not so bad and look at the horrible thing he did." Conversely, the argument might be: "These horrible things happened to the defendant and now he is damaged beyond repair" (that is, "irreparably corrupt"). Either way, the clinician's responses should incorporate the defendant's individual characteristics and circumstances, normal development for adolescents and young adults, and considerations in the particular case that can impact the normal developmental trajectory.

Be prepared for questions related to rehabilitation. In a sentencing case, the issue may be conceptualized as: "Is the defendant beyond rehabilitation?" For resentencing, the question might be: "Has the defendant been rehabilitated?" In either case, the clinician should remember that, according to *Miller*, the question is not only what evidence there is for rehabilitative progress, but also if there is further rehabilitative potential.

On cross-examination, the lowest-hanging fruit that the prosecution might try to employ is some version of this: "Most sixteen-year-olds who have [insert particular characteristics—e.g., smoked marijuana daily] do not go on to kill someone." In response, consider referencing base rates for the crime being committed by someone the defendant's age and reminding the court that you were retained to interview this particular defendant. You could then reiterate some of the variables, characteristics, or factors described in response to your opinion regarding the first, second, and perhaps the third *Miller* factors. Finally, in offering a clinical opinion about the *Miller* factors, your response could include a reminder that you are not attempting to excuse the defendant's behavior. Instead, you are attempting to place it in a developmental context consistent with the *Miller* holding.

CROSS-EXAMINATION BY DEFENSE ATTORNEY

On cross-examination, the defense attorney may pose questions aimed at increasing the weight or importance of some aspect of the defendant's life experiences beyond the importance given it by the clinician. For example, the report might state that the defendant has some symptoms often associated with a certain disorder, such as depression or schizophrenia. The attorney, however, might pose questions about the defendant's "diagnosis" of depression or schizophrenia. Posing questions in this manner may be strategic. The attorney is attempting to present his client as more impaired than may be the case. This strategy is at odds with your role, which involves describing accurately how impaired the youth was. It is important that the clinician testify in a manner that is consistent with the way the clinical opinion is conveyed in the report. While attorneys are advocating for their client, the role of clinicians is to advocate for their clinical opinion.

As an advocate, the defense attorney might ask a series of questions that involve viewing the report through an oversimplified or reductionist lens. In doing this, the attorney may attempt to make the events noted in the report more causal than correlated. Two examples help to illustrate this, both of which arise with some frequency.

One pertains to causal inferences regarding substance use. Imagine that the report notes that the defendant smokes marijuana routinely, but only on the weekend. The attorney might pose questions to suggest that marijuana usage "caused" the client to commit the offense, whereas no such opinion was expressed in the report. In responding to this line of questioning, remember that your testimony should reiterate and be consistent with what has been memorialized in the report. Highlighting the defendant's immaturity and youthfulness as if these are global traits is another form of oversimplification. In responding to this line of questioning, place these characteristics in context. In doing so, you might proffer testimony that provides an accurate picture of the youth's development.

Second, it is not uncommon for defense attorneys to magnify the impact of prior traumatic experience in a way that could benefit their client. They might ask questions that equate a traumatic experience with a current diagnosis of Post-Traumatic Stress Disorder. In this case, the clinician may note that not all traumatic experiences in childhood result in enduring trauma-related symptoms or conditions (e.g., Post-Traumatic Stress Disorder). Moreover, if such enduring symptoms do exist, they are best construed and described as contributing to the defendant's behavior rather than providing a causal explanation for the defendant's behavior. Causal inferences, which imply that "but for the condition, the behavior would not have occurred," typically are beyond our ability to infer with confidence.

Courts may expect the clinician to have offered an estimate of future risk of recidivism based on a risk assessment score. In responding to this line of questioning, be prepared to explain the limited value of an estimate of future risk of recidivism, especially as part of *Miller* or *de facto* life evaluations. In responding to this line of questioning, keep the following points in mind: (a) an estimate of future risk assessment is not cited among the *Miller* criteria, although (as discussed in Chapters 2 and 3) criminogenic needs are important; (b) you have identified areas that need to be addressed to increase the potential for rehabilitation; and (c), in the case of *Miller* or *de facto* life evaluations, assessing what risk a person will pose in 20, 40, or more years can be evaluated more accurately closer to when the defendant has a meaningful opportunity to rejoin the community. As has been discussed, in some resentencing cases where an imminent release into the community is likely, then an estimate of future risk of recidivism within the community could be appropriate.

Conclusion

Miller evaluations are not for the faint of heart. The stakes are high. The severity of the offenses represents a serious matter of public safety. The severity of the sentences is a serious matter for the future of our youth.

The demands on the expert for communicating the results and negotiating the legal inquiry are among the greatest in forensic mental health assessment. The quality of the evaluation requires extraordinary professional scope, including expertise in child clinical, developmental, and forensic matters—and, in *Miller* resentencing cases, adult clinical matters as well. The report must reflect high integrity, provide accurate and understandable information, and help the expert withstand the zeal with which both parties will make their arguments.

As if this were not enough pressure, consider also the relatively limited precedent. There is little published work (and this is the first book to date) focused exclusively on *Miller* evaluations, reports, and testimony. The clinical and forensic foundations of one's reports and testimony can be sound, but they are being applied to a relatively new legal issue: the potential reduced culpability of adolescents for the most serious crimes in society.

Clinicians who take up the challenge of *Miller* evaluations will find them demanding, stressful, and possibly exciting. But they should recognize that the manner in which they conduct and communicate them will influence the courts' expectations regarding what psychological forensic experts can provide. May clinicians proceed with an eye to their responsibilities to shape the future of *Miller* evaluations for the benefit of our profession, the legal system, the defendants who deserve fairness and accuracy, and our larger society.

Appendix

Template for *Miller* Reports

(An asterisk designates additional sections relevant to *resentencing* reports. When relevant local case law or statutes clarify or alter the *Miller* factors, cite those altered factors and the relevant statute or case.)

Forensic Evaluation

Identifying Information

Defendant:
Case number:
Date of birth:
Age at the time of the crime:
Age at the time of evaluation:
Years since arrest*:
Date of report:
Examiner:

Reason for Evaluation

Clinically Relevant Language from *Miller*

In *Miller v. Alabama*, the U.S. Supreme Court articulated factors that lower courts should consider when deciding a new sentence for those who had been automatically sentenced to life without parole for crimes they committed before their 18th birthday. Those factors to be considered include:

(1) *The Family and Home Environment.* The Court held, "[T]he family and home environment that surrounds him—from which he cannot usually extricate himself—no matter how brutal or dysfunctional." *Miller v. Alabama,* 132 S Ct. 2455, 2458 (2012).
(2) *The Offender's Age and Characteristics.* The Court held, "[T]he offender's age and the wealth of characteristics and circumstances attendant to it" are relevant factors. *Miller v. Alabama*, 132 S Ct. 2455, 2467 (2012). The Court recognized it is important to consider factors beyond the youth's age, such as the youth's thinking, level of impulsivity, and other characteristics and circumstances, including whether the youth had extended periods away from the primary caregiver; and the circumstances of the youth's delinquent/criminal history.
(3) *The Circumstances of the Offense.* "[T]he circumstances of the homicide offense, including the extent of his participation in the conduct and the way family and peer pressures may have affected him." *Miller v. Alabama*, 132 S. Ct. 2455, 2468 (2012).
(4) *Prospects for Rehabilitation.* The Supreme Court held that "mandatory punishment disregards the possibility of rehabilitation even when the circumstances most suggest it." *Miller v. Alabama*, 132 S Ct. 2455, 2468 (2012).

Sources of Data and Evaluation Techniques

Account of the Offense Based on Police and Court Records

Review of Relevant Records

Mental Status and Behavioral Observations

Relevant Interview Information Obtained from [insert names]

[Defendant's name]'s Account of the Offense

[Defendant's name]'s Account of Life in Prison*

Relevant Collateral Interview Information Obtained from [insert name of collateral] or Relevant Collateral Interview Information

Data from Testing and Specialized Measures

Best practices for psychologists dictate that diagnostic impressions are not based solely on test data and that test data are compared to the test taker's records (e.g., academic, mental health, criminal, vocational) to gauge if the interpretation applies to the test taker.

Clinical Opinion Regarding *Miller* Factors

In *Miller v. Alabama*, the Court articulated factors to be considered at a (re) sentencing hearing. This section of this report applies those clinically relevant factors to the case at hand.

(1) *The Family and Home Environment.* The Court held, "[T]he family and home environment that surrounds him—from which he cannot usually extricate himself—no

matter how brutal or dysfunctional." Miller v. Alabama, 132 S Ct. 2455, 2458 (2012).

(2) *The Offender's Age and Characteristics.* The Court held, "[T]he offender's age and the wealth of characteristics and circumstances attendant to it" are relevant factors. Miller v. Alabama, 132 S Ct. 2455, 2467 (2012). The Court recognized it is important to consider factors beyond the youth's age, such as the youth's thinking, level of impulsivity, and other characteristics and circumstances, including whether the youth had extended periods away from the primary caregiver; and the circumstances of the youth's delinquent/criminal history.

(3) *The Circumstances of the Offense.* "[T]he circumstances of the homicide offense, including the extent of his participation in the conduct and the way family and peer pressures may have affected him." Miller v. Alabama, 132 S. Ct. 2455, 2468 (2012).

(4) *Prospects for Rehabilitation.* The Supreme Court held that "mandatory punishment disregards the possibility of rehabilitation even when the circumstances most suggest it." Miller v. Alabama, 132 S Ct. 2455, 2468 (2012).

Respectfully submitted,
Expert's signature

Appendix: Records Reviewed

Legal References

Brown v. Precythe, Case No. 17-cv-4082. | 42 | 20190809c83 (W.D. Mo., 2017).

California Evidence Code 804.

Commonwealth v. Batts, No. 45 MAP 2016, 2017 WL 2735411 (Pa. June 26, 2017).

Graham v. Florida, 130 U.S. 2011 (2010).

In re Gault, 387 U.S. 1 (1967).

J.D.B. v. North Carolina, 131 U.S., 2394 (2011).

Jones v. Mississippi, Petition for a writ of certiorari filed March 29, 2019. Petition granted, March 13, 2020. https://www.supremecourt.gov/DocketPDF/18/18-1259/94684/20190329124507004_No.-__%20Cert%20Petition.pdf

Kent v. U.S., 383 U.S. 541 (1966).

McGee v. State, No. F-2015–393 (Okla. Crim. App. Dec. 2, 2016).

McKinley v. Butler, Case No. 14–1944, 1 /4/16 (7th Cir. 2016).

Miller v. Alabama, 132 S. Ct. 2455 (2012).

Montgomery v. Louisiana, 136 S. Ct. 718 (2016).

People v. Gutierrez, 324 P.3d 245 (Cal. 2014).

People v. Harris, 70 N.E.3d 718 (3rd Cir. 2016).

People v. House, No. 1-11-0580, 2015 WL 9428803 (3rd Cir. Dec. 24, 2015).

People v. Lozano, No. NA023984 (2nd Appellate District, Los Angeles County Super. Ct. (2016).*People v. Sanchez*, 63 Cal.4th 665 (Cal. 2016).

Roper v. Simmons, 125 U.S. 1183 (2005).

Sharp v. State, 16 N.E.3d 470 (Ind. App. Ct. 2014), transfer granted, opinion vacated, 37 N.E.3d 961 (Ind. 2015), and vacated, 42 N.E.3d 512 (Ind. 2015).

State v. Bassett, Docket No. 94556-0 (Wash. October 18, 2018).

State v. Null, 836 N.W.2d 41 (Iowa 2013).

State v. O'Dell, 358 P.3d 359 (Wash. 2015).

State v. Ragland, 836 N.W.2d 107 (Iowa 2013).

State v. Ramos, 32027-8 (Wash. Ct. App. 2015).

State v. Seats, 865 N.W.2d 545 (Iowa 2015).

State v. Valencia, 370 P.3d 124 (Ariz. 2016).

United States v. Briones, No. 16-10150 (July 9, 2019, 9th Cir.).

Veal v. State, 784 S.E.2d 403 (Ga. 2016).

White v. Premo, (CC 11C24315) (CA A154435) (SC S065188) (Or. 2019).

References

Abram, K., Teplin, L., Charles, D., Longworth, S., McClelland, G., Dulcan, M., Achenbach, T., & Rescorla, L. (2004). Posttraumatic stress disorder and trauma in youth in juvenile detention. *Archives of General Psychiatry, 61*, 403–410.

Abram, K., Teplin, L., King, D., Longworth, S., Emanuel, K., Romero, E., McClelland, G., Dulcan, M., Washburn, J., Welty, L., & Olson, M., (2013). *PTSD, trauma, and comorbid psychiatric disorders in detained youth.* Washington, DC: Office of Juvenile Justice and Delinquency Prevention.

Ackerman, M. J. (2010). *Essentials of forensic psychological assessment* (2nd ed.). Hoboken, NJ: John Wiley & Sons Inc.

Ahonen, L., Loeber, R., & Pardini, D. (2015). The prediction of young homicide and violent offenders. *Justice Quarterly, 33*, 1265–1291.

Alexander, J., Pugh, C., & Parsons, B. (1998). Functional family therapy. In D. Elliott (Ed.), *Blueprints for violence prevention* (Vol. 2, Book 3, pp. 13–47). Boulder, CO: University of Colorado, Institution of Behavioral Science.

Allen, L. C., MacKenzie, D. L., & Hickman, L. J. (2001). The effectiveness of cognitive behavioral treatment for adult offenders: A methodological, quality-based review. *International Journal of Offender Therapy and Comparative Criminology, 45*, 498–514.

American Academy of Psychiatry and the Law. (2005). *Ethical guidelines for the practice of forensic psychiatry.* Retrieved November 20, 2019, from http://www.aapl.org/ethics-guidelines.

American Bar Association. (2019). *Model rules of professional conduct* (2019 ed.). Chicago, IL: Center for Professional Responsibility, American Bar Association.

American Psychiatric Association. (2013). *Diagnostic and statistical manual of mental disorders* (5th ed.). Arlington, VA: American Psychiatric Association.

American Psychological Association. (2007). *Statement on third-party observers in psychological testing and assessment: A framework for decision making.* Retrieved November 8, 2019, from https://www.apa.org/science/programs/testing/third-party-observers.pdf.

American Psychological Association. (2012). Brief for the American Psychological Association, American Psychiatric Association, and National Association of Social Workers as Amici Curiae. *In Support of Petitioners: In the United States Supreme Court, Miller v. Alabama and Jackson v. Hobbs.* https://www.apa.org/about/offices/ogc/amicus/index-issues.aspx.

American Psychological Association. (2013). Specialty guidelines for forensic psychology. *American Psychologist, 68*, 7–19.

American Psychological Association. (2019). *APA guidelines on race and ethnicity in psychology: Promoting responsiveness and equity.* Retrieved November 20, 2019, from http://www.apa.org/about/policy/race-and-ethnicity-in-psychology.pdf.

Andersheid, H., Gustafson, S, Kerr, M., & Stattin, H. (2002). The usefulness of self-reported psychopathy-like traits in the study of antisocial behavior among non-referred adolescents. *European Journal of Personality, 16*, 383–402.

Andrews, D., & Bonta, J. (2017). *The psychology of criminal conduct* (6th ed.). New York, NY: Routledge.

Andrews, D., Bonta, J., & Wormith, J. (2004). *Level of Service/Case Management Inventory (LS/CMI)*. North Tonawanda, NY: Multi-Health Systems Inc.

Andrews, A., & Dowden, C. (2005). Managing correctional treatment for reduced recidivism: A meta-analytic review of program integrity. *Legal and Criminological Psychology, 19*, 173–187.

Andrews, D. A., Zinger, I., Hoge, R., Bonta, J., Gendreau, P., & Cullen, F., (1990). Does correctional treatment work? A clinically relevant and psychologically informed meta-analysis. *Criminology, 28, 369*–404.

Armstrong, J. G., Putnam, F. W., Carlson, E. B., Libero, D. Z., & Smith, S. R. (1997). Development and validation of a measure of adolescent dissociation: The Adolescent Dissociative Experiences Scale. *Journal of Nervous and Mental Disease, 185*, 491–497.

Arnold, S., Flack, D., & Heilbrun, K. (2018). Risk assessment and juvenile sentencing: A critical analysis. *Behavioral Sciences & the Law, 36*, 576–586.

Baglivio, M., Epps, N., Swartz, K., Huq, M., Sheer, A., & Hardt, N. (2014). The prevalence of adverse childhood experiences (ACE) in the lives of juvenile offenders. *Journal of Juvenile Justice, 3*, 1–17.

Baglivio, M., & Wolff, K. (2017). Prospective prediction of juvenile homicide/attempted homicide among early-onset juvenile offenders. *International Journal of Environmental Research and Public Health, 14*, 197.

Bechara, A., Damasio, A., Damasio, H., & Anderson, S. (1994). Insensitivity to future consequences following damage to human prefrontal cortex. *Cognition, 50*, 7–15.

Bechtold, J., & Cauffman, E. (2014). Tried as an adult, housed as a juvenile: A tale of youth from two courts incarcerated together. *Law and Human Behavior, 38*, 126–138.

Becker, S., & Kerig, P. (2011). Post-traumatic stress disorder symptoms are associated with the frequency and severity of delinquency among detained boys. *Journal of Clinical Child and Adolescent Psychology, 40*, 765–771.

Ben-Porath, Y. S. (2012). *Interpreting the MMPI-2-RF.* Minneapolis, MN: University of Minnesota Press.

Ben-Porath, Y., & Tellegen, A. (2008). *Minnesota Multiphasic Personality Inventory-2-Restructured Form: Manual for administration, scoring and interpretation*. Minneapolis, MN: University of Minnesota Press.

Benedek, E., & Cornell, D. (1990). *Juvenile homicide*. Washington, DC: American Psychiatric Press.

Benner, A., Wang, Y., Shen, Y., Boyle, A., Polk, R., & Cheng, Y. (2018). Racial/ethnic discrimination and well-being during adolescence: A meta-analytic review. *American Psychologist*, *73*, 855–883.

Benthin, A., Slovic, P., & Seveerson, H. (1993). A psychometric study of adolescent risk perception. *Journal of Adolescence*, *16*, 153–168.

Berg, W., & Byrd, D. (2002). The Tower of London spatial problem solving task: Enhancing clinical and research implementation. *Journal of Experimental and Clinical Neuropsychology*, *25*, 586–604.

Bersani, B., & Doherty, E. (2018). Desistance from offending in the twenty-first century. *Annual Review of Criminology*, *1*, 311–334.

Bersani, B., Nieuwbeerta, P., & Laub, J. (2009). Predicting trajectories of offending over the life course from a Dutch conviction cohort. *Journal of Research in Crime and Delinquency*, *46*, 468–494.

Boone, B. (2015). Treating adults like children: Resentencing adult juvenile lifers after *Miller v. Alabama*. *Minnesota Law Review*, *99*, 1159–1194.

Borum, R., Bartel, P., & Forth, A. (2006). *Manual for the Structured Assessment for Violence Risk in Youth (SAVRY)*. Odessa, FL: Psychological Assessment Resources.

Borum, R., Bartel, P., & Forth, A. (in press). Structured assessment of violence risk in youth. In K. S. Douglas & R. K. Otto (Eds.), *Handbook of violence risk assessment* (2nd ed., pp. _____). New York, NY: Taylor and Francis.

Briere, J. (1996). *Trauma symptom checklist for children: Professional manual*. Odessa, FL: Psychological Assessment Resources.

Brodsky, S. L., & Gutheil, T. G. (2016). *The expert expert witness: More maxims and guidelines for testifying in court* (2nd ed.). Washington, DC: American Psychological Association.

Brodsky, S. L., Wilson, J. K., & Neal, T. M. S. (2013). Refusing and withdrawing from forensic evaluations. *Journal of Forensic Psychology Practice*, *13*(1), 14–26. Retrieved November 8, 2019, from http://ezproxy.lib.usf.edu/login?url=http://search.ebscohost.com/login.aspx?direct=true&db=edsbl&AN=RN325604807&site=eds-live.

Bronson, J., & Berzofsky, M. (2017). *Indicators of mental health problems reported by prisoners and jail inmates, 2011–12*. Washington, DC: U.S. Department of Justice. Retrieved November 8, 2019, from https://www.bjs.gov/content/pub/pdf/imprpji1112.pdf.

Buckley, L., Broadley, M., & Cascio, C. (2019). Socio-economic status and the developing brain in adolescence: A systematic review. *Child Neuropsychology*, *25*, 859–884.

Burrell, S., & Warboys, L. (2000). *Special education and the juvenile justice system*. Washington, DC: Office of Juvenile Justice and Delinquency Prevention.

Butts, J., & Travis, J. (2002). *The rise and fall of American youth violence*. Washington, DC: Urban Institute. Retrieved November 8, 2019, from. https://www.urban.org/sites/default/files/publication/60381/410437-The-Rise-and-Fall-of-American-Youth-Violence.PDF.

Caldwell, J., Skeem, J., Salekin, R., & van Rybroek, G. (2006). Treatment response of adolescent offenders with psychopathy features: A two-year follow-up. *Criminal Justice and Behavior*, *33*, 571–596.

Campaign for the Fair Sentencing of Youth. (2018). *States that ban life without parole for children*. Retrieved November 8, 2019, from https://www.fairsentencingofyouth.org/media-resources/states-that-ban-life/.

Caudill, W., & Trulson, R. (2016). The hazards of premature release: Recidivism outcomes of blended-sentenced juvenile homicide offenders. *Journal of Criminal Justice*, *46*, 219–227.

Cauffman, E., Skeem, J., Dmitrieva, J., & Caitlin, C. (2016). Comparing the stability of psychopathy scores in adolescents versus adults: How often is "fledgling psychopathy" misdiagnosed? *Psychology Public Policy and Law*, *22*, 77–91.

Chein, J., O'Brien, A., Uchert, K., & Steinberg, L. (2011). Peers increase adolescent risk taking by enhancing activity in the brain's reward circuitry. *Developmental Science*, *14*, 1–10.

Cicchetti, D. (1984). The emergence of developmental psychopathology. *Child Development*, *55*, 1–7.

Cicchetti, D., & Rogosch, F. (2002). A developmental psychopathology perspective on adolescence. *Journal of Consulting and Clinical Psychology*, *70*, 6–20.

Clauss-Ehlers, C. S., Chiriboga, D. A., Hunter, S. J., Roysircar, G., & Tummala-Narra, P. (2019). APA multicultural guidelines executive summary: Ecological approach to context, identity, and intersectionality. *American Psychologist*, *74*(2), 232–244.

Cleckley, H. (1976). *The mask of sanity*. New York: C.V. Mosby Co.

Cohen, A., Breiner, K., Steinberg, L., Bonnie, R., Scott, E., Taylor-Thompson, K., Rudolph, M., Chein, J., Richeson, J., Heller, A., Silverman, M., Dellarco, D., Fair, D., Galvan, A., & Casey, B. (2016). When is an adolescent an adult? Assessing cognitive control in emotional and nonemotional contexts. *Psychological Science*, *27*, 49–62.

Cole, E. R. (2009). Intersectionality and research in psychology. *American Psychologist*, *64*(3), 170–180.

Commons, M. L., Miller, P. M., Li, E. Y., & Gutheil, T. G. (2012). Forensic experts' perceptions of expert bias. *International Journal of Law & Psychiatry*, *35*, 362–371.

Cornell, D., Benedek, E., & Benedek, D. (1987). Juvenile homicide: Prior adjustment and a proposed typology. *American Journal of Orthopsychiatry, 57*, 383–393.

Cornell, D., Warren, J., Hawk, G., Stafford, E., Oram, G., & Pine, D. (1996). Psychopathy in instrumental and reactive violent offenders. *Journal of Consulting and Clinical Psychology, 64*, 783–790.

Crenshaw, K. (1989). Demarginalizing the intersection of race and sex: A black feminist critique of antidiscrimination doctrine, feminist theory and antiracist politics. *University of Chicago Legal Forum, 1989*(1). Retrieved November 8, 2019, from http://chicagounbound.uchicago.edu/uclf/vol1989/iss1/8.

Cruise, K. R., Morin, S. L., & Affleck, K. (2016). Residential interventions with justice involved youths. In K. Heilbrun, D. DeMatteo, & N.S. Goldstein (Eds.), *APA handbook of psychology and juvenile justice* (pp. 611–639). Washington, DC: American Psychological Association.

Culbertson, W., & Zillmer, E. (2005). *Tower of London- Drexel University* (2nd ed.) Toronto: Multi-Health Systems.

Cunningham, M. (2010). *Evaluation for capital sentencing.* New York, NY: Oxford University Press.

Cunningham, M. D., Reidy, T. J., & Sorensen, J. R. (2008). Assertions of "future dangerousness" at federal capital sentencing: Rates and correlates of subsequent prison misconduct and violence. *Law & Human Behavior, 32*(1), 46–63.

Cunningham, M. D., & Sorensen, J. R. (2006). Nothing to lose? A comparative examination of prison misconduct rates among life-without-parole and other long-term high-security inmates. *Criminal Justice and Behavior, 33*(6), 683–705.

Davis, M., & Vander Stoep, A. (1997). The transition to adulthood for youth who have serious emotional disturbance: Developmental transition and young adult outcomes. *Journal of Mental Health Administration, 24*, 400–427.

DeMatteo, D., Edens, J., & Hart, S. (2010). The use of measures of psychopathy in violence risk assessment. In R. Otto & K. Doulas (Eds.), *Handbook of violent risk assessment* (pp. 19–40). New York, NY: Routledge.

DeMatteo, D., Wollansky, M., & LaDuke, C. (2016). Risk assessment with juveniles. In K. Heilbrun, D. DeMatteo, & N. S. Goldstein (Eds.), *APA handbook of psychology and juvenile justice* (pp. 365–384). Washington, DC: American Psychological Association.

DeMier, R. L., & Otto, R. K. (2017). Forensic report writing: Principles and challenges. In R. Roesch & A. N. Cook (Eds.), *Handbook of forensic mental health services* (pp. 216–234). New York, NY: Routledge/Taylor & Francis Group.

DeRight, J., & Carone, D. A. (2015). Assessment of effort in children: A systematic review. *Child Neuropsychology, 21*(1), 1–24.

Desai, R., Falzer, P. R., Chapman, J., & Borum, R. (2012). Mental illness, violence risk, and race in juvenile detention: Implications for disproportionate minority contact. *American Journal of Orthopsychiatry*, *82*(1), 32–40.

DiCataldo, F., & Everett, M. (2008). Distinguishing juvenile homicide from violent juvenile offending. *International Journal of Offender Therapy and Comparative Criminology*, *52*, 158–174.

DiCataldo, F., Linder, C., Neddenriep, J., Domas, S., Christensen, M., & Kinscherff, R. (2017). The recidivism of juveniles convicted of homicide and released as adults. *Today's Children-Tomorrow's Parents*, *45*, 87–101.

Dierkhising, C., Ko, S., Woods-Jaeger, N. Briggs, E., Lee, R., & Pynoos, S. (2013). Trauma histories among justice-involved youth: Findings from the National Child Traumatic Stress *Network, European Journal of Psychotraumatology*, *4*, 10.

Dierkhising, C. B., Lane, A., & Natsuaki, M. N. (2014). Victims behind bars: A preliminary study of abuse during juvenile incarceration and post-release social and emotional functioning. *Psychology, Public Policy, and Law*, *20*, 181–190.

Douglas, K. S., Hart, S. D., Webster, C. D., & Belfrage, H. (2013). *HCR-20V3: Assessing risk of violence—User guide*. Burnaby, Canada: Mental Health, Law, and Policy Institute, Simon Fraser University.

Douglas, K. S., & Shaffer-McCuish, C. S. (in press). The Historical-Clinical-Risk Management 20, Version 3 (HCR-20 V3): Overview, research, and applications. In K. S. Douglas & R. K. Otto (Eds.), *Handbook of violence risk assessment* (2nd ed., pp. _____). New York, NY: Taylor and Francis.

Drogin, E. Y., Commons, M. L., Gutheil, T. G., Meyer, D. J., & Norris, D. M. (2012). "Certainty" and expert mental health opinions in legal proceedings. *International Journal of Law and Psychiatry*, *35*(5-6), 348–353.

Dumontheil, I., Wolf, L., & Blakemore, S. (2016). Audience effects on the neural correlates of relational reasoning in adolescence. *Neuropsychologia*, *1*, 85–95.

Durose, M., Cooper, A., & Snyder, H. (2014). *Recidivism of prisoners released in 30 states in 2005: Patterns from 2005 to 2010*. Washington, DC: U.S. Department of Justice, Office of Justice Programs, Bureau of Justice Statistics.

Duwe, G. (2017). *The use and impact of correctional programming for inmates on pre- and post-release outcomes*. Washington, DC: National Institute of Justice.

Duwe, G., & Clark, V. (2015). Importance of program integrity: Outcome evaluation of a gender-responsive, cognitive-behavioral program for female offenders. *Criminology & Public Policy*, *14*, 301–328.

Edens, J., Skeem, J., Cruise, K., & Cauffman, E. (2001). Assessment of "juvenile psychopathy" and its association with violence: A critical review. *Behavioral Sciences & the Law, 19*, 53–80.

Edens, J. F., Smith, S. T., Magyar, M. S., Mullen, K., Pitta, A., & Petrila, J. (2012). "Hired guns," "charlatans," and their "voodoo psychobabble": Case law references to various forms of perceived bias among mental health expert witnesses. *Psychological Services, 9*(3), 259–271.

Edwards, J. H., & Rogers, K. C. (1997). The Traumatic Events Screening Inventory: Assessing trauma in children. In G. Kantor & J. L. Jasinski (Eds.), *Out of darkness: Contemporary perspectives on family violence* (pp. 113–118). Thousand Oaks, CA: Sage.

Epstein, E. S. (2014). Deposition preparation: The four simple rules all clients, even sophisticated ones, need to be told how to achieve a successful deposition. *Litigation Magazine, 40*(4).

Erikson, E. H. (1993). *Childhood and society.* New York, NY: WW Norton & Company.

Ewing, C. (1990). *When children kill: Dynamics of juvenile homicide.* Lexington, MA: Lexington Books.

Fairfax-Columbo, J., Fishel, S., & DeMatteo, D. (2019). Distinguishing "incorrigibility" from "transient immaturity:" Risk assessment in the context of sentencing/resentencing evaluations of juvenile homicide offenders. *Translational Issues in Psychological Science, 5*, 132–142.

Farrington, D. (1986). Age and crime. *Crime and Justice, 7*, 189–250.

Farrington, D. (2005). Introduction to integrate developmental and life-course theories of offending. In D. Farrington (Ed.), *Advances in criminological theory: Vol. 14: Integrated developmental and life course theories of offending* (pp. 1–14). Brunswick, NJ: Transaction Publishers.

Farrington, D. (2008). *Integrated developmental and life-course theories of offending.* Brunswick, NJ: Routledge.

Federal Bureau of Investigation. (2013). *Crime in the United States, 2012.* Retrieved November 8, 2019, from http://www.fbi.gov/about-us/cjis/ncr/crime-in-tthe-u.s/2012/crime-in-the-u.s.-2012.

Federal Rules of Evidence. (2019). Grand Rapids, MI: Michigan Legal Publishing Ltd.

Finkelhor, D., Hamby, S. L., Ormrod, R., & Turner, H. (2005). The Juvenile Victimization Questionnaire: Reliability, validity, and national norms. *Child Abuse & Neglect, 29*, 383–412.

Ford, J., Chapman, J., Mack, J., & Pearson, G. (2006). Pathways from traumatic child victimization to delinquency: Implications for juvenile and permanency court proceedings and decisions. *Juvenile and Family Court Journal, 57*, 13–26.

Forth, A., Kosson, D., & Hare, R. (2003). *The Psychopathy Checklist: Youth Version manual.* Toronto, Ontario, Canada: Multi-Health Systems.

Frick, P. (2004). *The Inventory of Callous-Unemotional Traits.* Unpublished rating scale.

Frick, P., & Hare, R. (2001). The *Antisocial Process Screening Devise*. Toronto, Ontario, Canada: Multi-Health Systems.

Frick, P., & White, S. (2008). Research review: The importance of callous-unemotional traits for the development of aggressive and antisocial behavior. *Journal of Child Psychology and Psychiatry, 49*, 359–375.

Gilman, A. B., Hill, K. G., Hawkins, J. D., Howell, J. C., & Kosterman, R. (2014). The developmental dynamics of joining a gang in adolescence: Patterns and predictors of gang membership. *Journal of Research on Adolescence, 24*(2), 204–219. doi:10.1111/jora.12121

Glaser, J., Martin, K. D., & Kahn, K. B. (2015). Possibility of death sentence has divergent effect on verdicts for black and white defendants. *Law and Human Behavior, 39*(6), 539–546. doi:10.1037/lhb0000146

Golden, C. (1978). *Stroop Color and Word Test: Manual for clinical and experimental uses*. Chicago, IL: Stoetling.

Gonzales, J., & Connell, M. (2014). Mental health of prisoners: Identifying barriers to mental health treatment and medication continuity. *American Journal of Public Health, 104*, 23228–23233.

Gottfredson, M. (2003). *Control theories of crime and delinquency*. Brunswick, NJ: Routledge.

Gottfredson, M., & Hirschi, T. (1990). *A general theory of crime*. Stanford, CA: Stanford University Press.

Gottfried, E. D., & Christopher, S. C. (2017). Mental disorders among criminal offenders: A review of the literature. *Journal of Correctional Health Care, 23*(3), 336–346.

Green, L., Myerson, J., & Ostaszewsk, P. (1999). Discounting of delayed rewards across the life span: age differences in individual discounting functions. *Behavioral Processes, 46*, 89–96.

Greenberger, E., & Sorensen, A. (1974). Toward a concept of psychological maturity. *Journal of Youth and Adolescence, 3*, 329–358.

Grisso, T. (1996). Society's retributive response to juvenile violence: A developmental perspective. *Law and Human Behavior, 20*, 229–247.

Grisso, T. (2004). *Double jeopardy: Juvenile offenders with mental disorders*. Chicago, IL: University of Chicago Press.

Grisso, T. (2005). *Evaluating juveniles' adjudicative competence: A guide for clinical practice*. Sarasota, FL: Professional Resource Press.

Grisso, T. (2010). Guidance for improving forensic reports: A review of common errors. *Open Access Journal of Forensic Psychology, 2*, 102–115.

Grisso, T. (2013). *Forensic evaluation of juveniles* (2nd ed.). Sarasota, FL: Professional Resource Press.

Grisso, T., & Kavanaugh, A. (2016). Prospects for developmental evidence in juvenile sentencing based on *Miller v. Alabama*. *Psychology, Public Policy and Law, 22*, 235–249.

Grzanka, P. R., Santos, C. E., & Moradi, B. (2017). Intersectionality research in counseling psychology. *Journal of Counseling Psychology, 64*(5), 453–457.

Hagan, M. (1997). An analysis of adolescent perpetrators of homicide and attempted homicide upon return to the community. *International Journal of Offender Therapy and Comparative Criminology*, *41*, 250–259.

Hamilton, M. N. (2018). The end of smuggling hearsay: How *People v. Sanchez* redefined the scope of expert basis testimony in California and beyond. *Chapman Law Review*, *21*(2), 509–544.

Haneveld, E., Neumann, C., Smid, W., Wever, E., & Kamphus, J. (2018). Treatment responsiveness of replicated psychopathy profiles. *Law and Human Behavior*, *42*, 484–495.

Haney, C. (2003). Psychological impact of incarceration: Implications for post-prison adjustment. In J. Travis & M. Waul (Eds.), *Prisoners once removed: The impact of incarceration and reentry on children, families and communities* (pp. 33–66). Washington, DC: Urban Institute Press.

Hart, S. (1998). The role of psychopathy in assessing risk for violence: Conceptual and methodological issues. *Legal and Criminological Psychology*, *3*, 121–140.

Hawes, D., Price, J., & Dadds, M. (2014). Callous-unemotional traits and the treatment of conduct problems in childhood and adolescence: A comprehensive review. *Clinical Child and Family Psychology Review*, *17*, 248–267.

Heide, K. (1992). *Why kids kill parents.* Columbus, OH: Ohio State University Press.

Heide, K., & Petee, T. (2007). Parricide: An empirical analysis of 24 years of U.S. data. *Journal of Interpersonal Violence*, *22*, 1382–1399.

Heide, K., Roe-Sepowitz, D., Soloman, E., & Choon, H. (2012). Male and female juveniles arrested for murder: A comprehensive analysis of U.S. data by offender gender. *International Journal of Offender Therapy and Comparative Criminology*, *56*, 356–384.

Heide, K., & Sellers, B. (2014). Girls arrested for murder: An empirical analysis of 32 years of U.S. data on offender age groups. *Behavioral Sciences & the Law*, *32*, 467–482.

Heide, K., Spencer, E., Thompson, A., & Solomon, E. (2001). Who's in, who's out, and who's back: Follow-up data on 59 juveniles incarcerated in adult prison for murder or attempted murder in the early 1980s. *Behavioral Sciences & the Law*, *19*, 97–108.

Heilbrun, K. (2001). *Principles of forensic mental health assessment.* New York, NY: Kluwer Academic/Plenum.

Heilbrun, K., DeMatteo, D., Brooks Holliday, S., & LaDuke, C. (2014). *Forensic mental health assessment: A casebook* (2nd ed.). New York, NY: Oxford University Press.

Heilbrun, K., DeMatteo, D., King, C., & Filone, S. (2017). *Evaluating juvenile transfer and disposition: Law, science, and practice.* New York, NY: Routledge.

Heilbrun, K., Grisso, T., & Goldstein, A. (2009). *Foundations of forensic mental health assessment.* New York, NY: Oxford University Press.

Heilbrun, K., Lee, R., & Cottle, C. C. (2005). Risk factors and intervention outcomes: Meta-analyses of juvenile offending. In K. Heilbrun, N. S. Goldstein, & R. Redding (Eds.), *Juvenile delinquency: Prevention, assessment, and intervention* (pp. 111–133). New York, NY: Oxford University Press.

Henggeler, S. W. (2016). Community-based interventions for juvenile offenders. In K. Heilbrun, D. DeMatteo, & N. E. S. Goldstein (Eds.), *APA handbook of psychology and juvenile justice* (pp. 575–595). Washington, DC: American Psychological Association.

Henggeler, S., Schoenwald, S., Borduin, C., Rowland, M., & Cunningham, P. (2009). *Multisystemic therapy for antisocial behavior in children and adolescents* (2nd ed.). New York, NY: Guilford Press.

Hirschi, T. (2002). *Causes of delinquency.* Piscataway, NJ: Transaction Publishers.

Hoge, R. (2016). Risk, need and responsivity in juveniles. In K. Heilbrun, D. DeMatteo, & N. E. S. Goldstein (Eds.), *APA handbook of psychology and juvenile justice* (pp. 177–196). Washington, DC: American Psychological Association.

Hoesterey, A. (2017). Confusion in *Montgomery*'s wake: State responses, the mandates of *Montgomery*, and why a complete categorical ban on life without parole for juveniles is the only constitutional option. *Fordham Urban Law Journal, 45*, 149–199.

Hoge, R., & Andrews, D. (2010). *Youth Level of Service/Case Management Inventory 2.0 (YLS/CMI) users' manual.* North Tonawanda, NY: Multi-Health Systems.

Icenogle, G., Steinberg, L., Duell, N., Chang, L., Chaudhary, N., Giunta, L., Dodge, K., Fanti, K., Lansford, J., Oburu, P., Pastorelli, C., Skinner, A., Sebring, E., Tapanya, S., Tirado, L., Alampay, L., Hassan, S., Takash, H., & Bacchini, D. (2019). Adolescents' cognitive capacity reaches adult levels prior to their psychosocial maturity: Evidence for a "maturity gap" in a multinational, cross-sectional sample. *Law and Human Behavior, 43*, 69–85.

Jenkins, E., & Bell, C. (1997). Adolescent violence: Can it be curbed? *Adolescent Medicine: State of the Art Reviews, 1*, 71–86.

Jolliffe, D., Farrington, D., Piquero, A., Loeber, R., & Mills, K. (2017). Systematic review of early risk factors for life-course-persistent, adolescence-limited, and late-onset offenders in prospective longitudinal studies. *Aggression and Violent Behavior, 33*, 15–23.

Kahn, L., Peake, S., Dission, T., Stormshak, E., & Pfeifer, J. (2015). Learning to play it safe (or not): Stable and evolving neural responses during adolescent risky decision-making. *Journal of Cognitive Neuroscience, 27*, 13–25.

Kahneman, D. (2013). *Thinking fast and slow.* New York: MacMillan.

Karson, M. (2015). What can the rules of evidence teach us about writing forensic reports? *Psychological Injury and Law*, *8*(1), 1–10.

Karson, M., & Karson, M., & Nadkarni, L. (2013)., L. (2013). *Principles of forensic report writing*. Washington, DC: American Psychological Association.

Kassin, S., Drizin, S., Grisso, T., Gudjonsson, G., Leo, R., & Redlich, A. (2010). Police-induced confessions: Risk factors and recommendations. *Law and Human Behavior*, *34*, 3–38.

Kassin, S. M., Dror, I. E., & Kukucka, J. (2013). The forensic confirmation bias: Problems, perspectives, and proposed solutions. *Journal of Applied Research in Memory and Cognition*, *2*(1), 42–52. doi:10.1016/j.jarmac.2013.01.001

Kazdin, A. (2000). Adolescent development, mental disorders, and decision making of delinquent youths. In T. Grisso & R. Schwartz (Eds.), *Youth on trial: A developmental perspective on juvenile justice* (pp. 33–65). Chicago, IL: University of Chicago Press.

Khachatryan, N. (2015). *Thirty-year follow-up of juvenile homicide offenders*. Graduate Theses and Dissertations. http://scholarcommons.usf.edu/etd/5822.

Khachatryan, N., Heide, K., Hummel, E., Ingraham, M., & Rad, J. (2016). Examination of long-term postrelease outcomes of juvenile homicide offenders. *Journal of Offender Rehabilitation*, *55*, 503–524.

Khachatryan, N., Heide, K., & Rad, J., & Hummel, W. (2016). Post-incarceration recidivism of lone versus group juvenile homicide offenders. *Behavioral Sciences & the Law*, *34*, 709–725.

Kinscherff, R. (2016). Distinguishing and assessing treatment needs and amenability to rehabilitation. In K. Heilbrun, D. DeMatteo & N. E. S. Goldstein (Eds.), *APA handbook of psychology and juvenile justice* (pp. 385–404). Washington, DC: American Psychological Association.

Koehler, J., Losel, F., Akoensi, T., & Humphreys, D. (2013). A systematic review and meta-analysis of the effects of young offender treatment programs in Europe. *Journal of Experimental Criminology*, *9*, 19–43.

Kolivoski, K. M., & Shook, J. J. (2016). Incarcerating juveniles in adult prisons: Examining the relationship between age and prison behavior in transferred juveniles. *Criminal Justice and Behavior*, *43*(9), 1242–1259.

Kruh, I., & Grisso, T. (2009). *Evaluations of juveniles' competence to stand trial*. New York, NY: Oxford University Press.

Kuanliang, A., Sorensen, J., & Cunningham, M. (2008). Juveniles in an adult prison system: Rates of disciplinary misconduct and violence. *Criminal Justice and Behavior*, 35, 1186–1201.

Lahey, B., van Hulle, C., Waldman, I., Rodgers, J., Onofrio, B., Pedlow, S., & Keenan, K. (2006). Testing descriptive hypotheses regarding sex differences in the development of conduct problems and delinquency. *Journal of Abnormal Child Psychology*, *334*, 730–748.

Lamb, M., & Freund, A. (2010). *The handbook of life-span development.* Hoboken, NJ: John Wiley and Sons.

Lambie, I., & Randell, I. (2013). The impact of incarceration on juvenile offenders. *Clinical Psychology Review, 33*, 448–459.

Larson, K., & Grisso, T. (2016). Transfer and commitment of youth in the United States: Law, policy, and forensic practice. In K. Heilbrun, D. DeMatteo, & N. E. S. Goldstein (Eds.), *APA handbook of psychology and juvenile justice* (pp. 445–466). Washington, DC: American Psychological Association.

Laub, J., & Sampson, R. (2003). *Shared beginnings, divergent lives: Delinquent boys to age 70.* Cambridge, MA: Harvard University Press.

Lauritsen, J., & Laub, J. (2007). Understanding the link between victimization and offending: New reflections on an old idea. In J. Hough & M. Maxfield (Eds.), *Surveying crime in the 21st century* (pp. 55–75). St. Louis, MO: Criminal Justice Press.

Lehmann, P. (2018). Sentencing other people's children: The intersection of race, gender, and juvenility in the adult criminal court. *Journal of Crime and Justice, 41*, 553–572.

Levick, M., & Feierman, J. (2016). Children in the justice system: The legal framework. In K. Heilbrun, D. DeMatteo, & N. E. S. Goldstein (Eds.), *APA handbook of psychology and juvenile justice* (pp. 23–43). Washington, DC: American Psychological Association.

Lewandowski, A., Baker, W. J., Sewick, B., Knippa, J., Axelrod, B., & McCaffrey, R. J. (2016). Policy statement of the American Board of Professional Neuropsychology regarding third party observation and the recording of psychological test administration in neuropsychological evaluations. *Applied Neuropsychology: Adult, 23*(6), 391–398. doi:http://dx.doi.org/10.1080/23279095.2016.1176366.

Lewis, J. A., & Grzanka, P. R. (2016). Applying intersectionality theory to research on perceived racism. In A. N. Alvarez, C. T. H. Liang, & H. A. Neville (Eds.), *The cost of racism for people of color: Contextualizing experiences of discrimination.* (pp. 31–54). Washington, DC: American Psychological Association.

Lin, L., Stamn, K., & Christidis, P. (2018). How diverse is the psychology workforce? *Monitor on Psychology, 49*, 19.

Lipsey, M. (2009). The primary factors that characterize effective interventions with juvenile offenders: A meta-analytic overview. *Victims and Offenders, 4*, 124–147.

Lipsey, J., Chapman, G., & Landenberger, N. (2001). Cognitive-behavioral programs for offenders. *Annals of the American Academy of Political and Social Science, 578*, 144–157.

Lipsey, M. W., Landenberger, N. A., & Wilson, S. J. (2007). Effects of cognitive-behavioral programs for criminal offenders: A systematic review. *Campbell Systematic Reviews, 6.* https://campbellcollaboration.org/media/k2/attachments/1028_R.pdf.

Loeber, R., Farrington, D., Hipwell, A., Stepp, S., Pardini, E., & Ahonen, L. (2015). Constancy and change in the prevalence and frequency of offending when based on longitudinal self-reports or official records: Comparisons by gender, race and crime type. *Journal of Developmental Life-Course Criminology, 1*, 150–168.

Loeber, R., Farrington, D., Stouthammer-Loeber, M., Moffitt, T., & Caspi, A. (1998). The development of male offending: Key findings from the first decade of the Pittsburgh Youth Study. *Studies in Crime and Crime Prevention, 7*, 141–172.

Loeber, R., Farrington, D., Stouthamer-Loeber, M., & van Kammen, W. (1998). *Antisocial behavior and mental health problems: Explanatory factors in childhood and adolescence.* Mahwah, NJ: Lawrence Erlbaum.

Loeber, R., Pardini, D., Homish, D., Wei, E., Crawford, A., Farrington, D., Stouthamer-Loeber, M., Creemers, J., Koehler, S., & Rosenfeld, R. (2005). The prediction of violence and homicide in young men. *Journal of Consulting and Clinical Psychology, 73*, 1074–1088.

Luna, B., & Wright, C. (2016). Adolescent brain development: Implications for the juvenile criminal justice system. In K. Heilbrun, D. DeMatteo, & N. E. S. Goldstein (Eds.), *APA handbook of psychology and juvenile justice* (pp. 91–116). Washington, DC: American Psychological Association.

Lynam, D., Caspi, A., Moffitt, T., Loeber, R., & Stouthamer-Loeber, M. (2007). Longitudinal evidence that psychopathy scores in early adolescence predict adult psychopathy. *Journal of Abnormal Psychology, 116*, 155–165.

Magat, J. A. (2010). Bottomheavy: Legal footnotes. *Journal of Legal Education, 60*(1), 65–105.

Maina, I. W., Belton, T. D., Ginzberg, S., Singh, A., & Johnson, T. J. (2018). A decade of studying implicit racial/ethnic bias in healthcare providers using the Implicit Association Test. *Social Science & Medicine, 199*, 219–229.

Maschi, T., Bradley, C., & Morgan, K. (2008). Unraveling the link between trauma and delinquency. *Youth Violence and Juvenile Justice, 6*, 136–157.

Mash, E., & Barkley, R. (Eds.). (2014). *Child psychopathology.* New York, NY: Guilford.

McDermott, B. (2012). Psychological testing and the assessment of malingering. *Psychiatric Clinics of North America, 35*, 855–876.

McDermott, B., & Sokolov, G. (2009). Malingering in a correctional setting: The use of the Structured Interview of Reported Symptoms in a jail sample. *Behavioral Science & the Law, 27*, 753–765.

Meade, B., & Steiner, B. (2010). The total effects of boot camps that house juveniles: A systematic review of the evidence. *Journal of Criminal Justice, 38*(5), 841–853.

Melton, G., Petrila, J., Poythress, N., Slobogin, C., Otto, R., Mossman, D., & Condie, L. (2018). *Psychological evaluations for the courts* (4th ed.). New York, NY: Guilford.

Miller, G. A. (2016). *The Substance Abuse Subtle Screening Inventory—Fourth Edition*. San Antonio, TX: Pearson Clinical Assessments.

Mills, J., Dorn, A., & Hritz, A. (2016). Juvenile life without parole in law and practice: Chronicling the rapid change underway. *American University Law Review, 65*, 535–605.

Millstein, S., & Halpern-Felsher, B. (2002). Perceptions of risk and vulnerability. *Journal of Adolescent Health, 31*, 10–27.

Mitchell, O., Wilson, D. B., & MacKenzie, D. L. (2007). Does incarceration-based drug treatment reduce recidivism? A meta-analytic synthesis of the literature. *Journal of Experimental Criminology, 3*, 353–375.

Moffitt, T. (1993). Adolescent-limited and life-course-persistent antisocial behavior: A developmental taxonomy. *Psychological Review, 100*, 674–701.

Moffitt, T. (2006). Life-course-persistent versus adolescence-limited antisocial behavior. In D. Cicchetti & D. Cohen (Eds.), *Handbook of developmental psychopathology* (pp. 570–598). Hoboken, NJ: Wiley.

Monahan, J. (1982). *The clinical prediction of violent behavior.* Rockville, MD: National Institute of Mental Health.

Monahan, K., Steinberg, L., Cauffman, E., & Mulvey, E. (2009). Trajectories of antisocial behavior and psychosocial maturity from adolescence to young adulthood. *Developmental Psychology, 45*, 1654–1668.

Morey, L. (1991). *The Personality Assessment Inventory: Professional manual.* Odessa, FL: Psychological Assessment Resources.

Mulvey, E. (2011). *Highlights from pathways to desistance: A longitudinal study of serious adolescent offenders.* Washington, DC: Office of Juvenile Justice and Delinquency Prevention. https://www.ncjrs.gov/pdffiles1/ojjdp/230971.pdf.

Mulvey, E., Steinberg, L., Fagan, J., Cauffman, E., Piquero, A., Chassin, T., Knight, G., Brame, R., Schubert, C., Hecker, T., & Losova, S. (2004). Theory and research on desistance from antisocial activity among serious adolescent offenders. *Youth Violence and Juvenile Justice, 2*, 213–236.

Mulvey, E., Steinberg, L., Piquero, A., Besana, M., Fagan, J., Schubert, C., & Cauffman, E. (2010). Trajectories of desistance and continuity in antisocial behavior following court adjudication among serious adolescent offenders. *Developmental Psychopathology, 22*, 453–475.

Murrie, D. C., Boccaccini, M. T., Guarnera, L. A., & Rufino, K. A. (2013). Are forensic experts biased by the side that retained them? *Psychological Science, 24*(10), 1889–1897.

Nagel, A., Guarnera, L., & Reppucci, N. (2016). Adolescent development, mental disorder, and decision making in delinquent youths. In K. Heilbrun, D. DeMatteo, & N. E. S. Goldstein (Eds.), *APA handbook of psychology and juvenile justice* (pp. 117–138). Washington, DC: American Psychological Association.

National Council on Disability. (2015). *Breaking the school-to-prison pipeline for students with disabilities.* Washington, DC: National Council on Disability.

National Council Medical Director Institute. (2017). *The psychiatric shortage: Causes and solutions.* Retrieved November 20, 2019, from https://www.thenationalcouncil.org/wp-content/uploads/2017/03/Psychiatric-Shortage_National-Council-.pdf.

National Institute of Corrections. (2017). *The problem of gangs and security threat groups (STGs) in American prisons and jails today: Recent findings from the 2012 NGCRC National Gang/STG survey.* https://nicic.gov/problem-gangs-and-security-threat-groups-stg%e2%80%99s-american-prisons-and-jails-today-recent-findings-2012.

National Institute of Justice. (2003). *Correctional boot camps: Lessons from a decade of research.* Washington, DC: U.S. Department of Justice Office of Justice Programs. Retrieved November 8, 2019, from https://www.ncjrs.gov/pdffiles1/nij/197018.pdf.

National Research Council. (2008). *Parole, desistance from crime, and community integration.* Washington, DC: The National Academies Press.

National Research Council of the National Academies. (2013). *Reforming juvenile justice: A developmental approach.* Washington, DC: National Academies Press.

Neal, T. M. (2016). Are forensic experts already biased before adversarial legal parties hire them? *PLOS One*, *11*(4), e0154434. doi:10.1371/journal.pone.0154434

Neal, T. M. S., & Grisso, T. (2014). The cognitive underpinnings of bias in forensic mental health evaluations. *Psychology, Public Policy, and Law*, *20*(2), 200–211.

Nellis, A. (2016). *The color of justice: Racial and ethnic disparity in state prisons.* Retrieved November 8, 2019, from https://www.sentencingproject.org/wp-content/uploads/2016/06/The-Color-of-Justice-Racial-and-Ethnic-Disparity-in-State-Prisons.pdf.

Nemeroff, C. (2004). Neurobiological consequences of childhood trauma. *Journal of Clinical Psychiatry*, *65*, 18–28.

Nosek, B., & Banaji, M. (2001). The Go/No-Go Association Task. *Social Cognition*, *19*, 161–176.

Odgers, C., Moffitt, T., Broadbent, J., Dickson, H., Hancox, R., Harrington, H., & Caspi, A. (2008). Female and male antisocial trajectories: From childhood origins to adult outcomes. *Development and Psychopathology*, *20*, 673–716.

Office of Juvenile Justice and Delinquency Prevention. (undated). *Model Program Guide.* https://www.ojjdp.gov/mpg.

Otto, R. K., DeMier, R. L., & Boccaccini, M. T. (2014). *Forensic reports and testimony: A guide to effective communication for psychologists and psychiatrists.* Hoboken, NJ: Wiley.

Packer, I. (2009). *Evaluation of criminal responsibility.* New York, NY: Oxford University Press.

Page, G., & Scalora, M. (2004). The utility of locus of control for assessing juvenile amenability to treatment. *Aggression and Violent Behavior, 9*, 523–534.

Patton, J., Stanford, M., & Barratt, E. (1995). Factor structure of the Barratt Impulsiveness Scale. *Journal of Clinical Psychology, 51, 768–774.*

Perry, S. P., Murphy, M. C., & Dovidio, J. F. (2015). Modern prejudice: Subtle, but unconscious? The role of bias awareness in whites' perceptions of personal and others' biases. *Journal of Experimental Social Psychology, 61*, 64–78.

Piaget, J., & Inhelder, B. (1955). *Growth of logical thinking.* London: Routledge.

Piquero, A. (2008). Taking stock of developmental trajectories of criminal activity over the life course. In A. Liberman (Ed.), *The long view of crime: A synthesis of longitudinal research* (pp. 23–78). Washington, DC: Springer.

Piquero, A. (2015). Understanding race/ethnicity differences in offending across the life span: Gaps and opportunities. *Journal of Developmental Life-Course Criminology, 1*, 21–32.

Piquero, A., Brame, R., & Moffitt, T. (2005). Extending the study of continuity and change: Gender differences in the linkage between adolescent and adult offending. *Journal of Quantitative Criminology, 21*, 219–243.

Piquero, A., Farrington, D., & Blumstein, (2003). The criminal career paradigm: Background and recent developments. In M. Tonry (Ed.), *Crime and justice: A review of research* (Vol. 30, pp. 359–506). Chicago, IL: University of Chicago Press.

Piquero, A., Jennings, W., & Barnes, J. (2012). Violence in criminal careers: A review of the literature from a developmental life-course perspective. *Aggression and Violent Behavior, 17*, 171–179.

Prins, S. J. (2014). Prevalence of mental illnesses in U.S. state prisons: A systematic review. *Psychiatric Services, 65*(7), 862–872.

Pronin, E., Lin, D. Y., & Ross, L. (2002). The bias blind spot: Perceptions of bias in self versus others. *Personality and Social Psychology Bulletin, 28*(3), 369–381.

Pynoos, R. S., Weathers, F. W., Steinberg, A. M., Marx, B. P., Layne, C. M., Kaloupek, D. G., Schnurr, P. P., Keane, T. M., Blake, D. D., Newman, E., Nader, K. O., & Kriegler, J. A. (2015). *Clinician-Administered PTSD Scale for DSM-5—Child/Adolescent Version.* Scale available from the National Center for PTSD at www.ptsd.va.gov.

Redding, R. E., Floyd, M. Y., & Hawk, G. L. (2001). What judges and lawyers think about the testimony of mental health experts: A survey of the courts and bar. *Behavioral Sciences & the Law*, *19*(4), 583–594.

Reidy, T., Sorensen, J., & Cunningham, M. (2012). Community violence to prison assault: A test of the behavioral continuity hypothesis. *Law and Human Behavior*, *36*, 356–363.

Reingle Gonzalez, J. M., & Connell., N. M. (2014). Mental health of prisoners: Identifying barriers to mental health treatment and medication continuity. *American Journal of Public Health*, *104*(12), 2328–2333.

Reyna, V., & Farley, F. (2006). Risk and rationality in adolescent decision-making: Implications for theory, practice, and public policy. *Psychological Science in the Public Interest*, *7*, 1–44.

Reynolds, C., & Kamphaus, R. (2015). *Behavior Assessment System for Children* (3rd ed.). San Antonio, TX: Pearson Clinical Assessment.

Richardson, G., Gudjonsson, G., & Kelly, T. (1995). Interrogative suggestibility in an adolescent forensic population. *Journal of Adolescence*, *18*(2), 211–216.

Riggs Romaine, C., & Kavanaugh, A. (2018). Risks, benefits and complexities: Reporting race and ethnicity in forensic mental health reports. *International Journal of Forensic Mental Health*, *8*, 138–152.

Rodway, C., Norrington-Moore, V., Appleby, L., & Shaw, J. (2011). An examination of the quality of psychiatric court reports for juvenile perpetrators of homicide. *Journal of Forensic Psychiatry & Psychology*, *22*(6), 895.

Rogers, R., & Ewing, C. P. (2003). The prohibition of ultimate opinions: A misguided enterprise. *Journal of Forensic Psychology Practice*, *3*(3), 65–75.

Rotter, J. (1966). Generalized expectancies for internal versus external control of reinforcement. *Psychological Monographs: General and Applied*, *8*, 1–28.

Russell, M., & Odgers, C. (2016). Desistance and life-course persistence: Findings from longitudinal studies using grou—based trajectory modeling of antisocial behavior. In K. Heilbrun, D. DeMatteo, & N. E. S. Goldstein (Eds.), *APA handbook of psychology and juvenile justice* (pp. 159–175). Washington, DC: American Psychological Association.

Salekin, R. (2004). *The Risk-Sophistication-Treatment Inventory: Professional manual*. Lutz, FL: Psychological Assessment Resources.

Salekin, R. (2015). *Forensic evaluation and treatment of juveniles: Innovation and best practice*. Washington, DC: American Psychological Association.

Salekin, R., Kubak, F., Lee, Z., Harrison, N., & Clark, A. (2018). Deception in children and adolescents. In R. Rogers & S. D. Bender (Eds.), *Clinical assessment of malingering and deception* (4th ed., pp. 475–496). New York, NY: Guilford Press.

Salekin, R., MacDougall, E., & Harrison, N. (2016). Developmental maturity and sophistication-maturity: Learning more about its purpose and assessment. In K. Heilbrun, D. DeMatteo, & N. E. S. Goldstein (Eds.), *APA handbook of psychology and juvenile justice* (pp. 405–424). Washington, DC: American Psychological Association.

Salekin, R., Rogers, R., & Ustad, K. (2001). Psychopathy in youth: Pursuing diagnostic clarity. *Journal of Youth and Adolescence*, *30*, 173–195.

Salekin, R., Tippey, J. G., & Allen, A. D. (2012). Treatment of conduct problem youth with interpersonal callous traits using mental models: Measurement of risk and change. *Behavioral Sciences & the Law*, *30*, 470–486.

Salekin, R., Yff, R., Neumann, C., Leistico, A., & Zalot, A. (2002). Juvenile transfer to adult court: A look at the prototypes for dangerousness, sophistication-maturity, and amenability to treatment through a legal lens. *Psychology, Public Policy and Law*, *8*, 373–410.

Sampson, R. (2012). Great *American city: Chicago and the enduring neighborhood effect*. Chicago: University of Chicago Press.

Sampson, R., & Laub, J. (2003). Life-course desisters? Trajectories of crime among delinquent boys followed to age 70. *Criminology*, *41*, 555–592.

Sattler, J. M. (2002). *Assessment of children: Behavioral and clinical applications* (4th ed.). La Mesa, CA: Sattler Publisher.

Sattler, J. (2008). *Assessment of children: Cognitive foundations*. La Mesa, CA: Sattler Publisher.

Schiess, W. (2014). *Writing for the legal audience* (2nd ed.). Durham, NC: Carolina Academic Press.

Schubert, C., Mulvey, E., & Glasheen, C. (2011). The influence of mental health and substance use problems and criminogenic risks on outcomes in serious juvenile offenders. *Journal of the American Academy of Child and Adolescent Psychiatry*, *50*, 925–937.

Scott, E., Grisso, T., Levick, M., & Steinberg, L. (2015). *The Supreme Court and the transformation of juvenile sentencing*. Chicago, IL: John D. and Catherine T. MacArthur Foundation. Retrieved November 8, 2019, from https://jlc.org/resources/supreme-court-and-transformation-juvenile-sentencing.

Scott, E., Grisso, T., Levick, M., & Steinberg, L. (2016). Juvenile sentencing reform in a constitutional framework. *Temple Law Review*, *88*, 675–716.

Scott, E., & Steinberg, L. (2008). *Rethinking juvenile justice*. Cambridge, MA: Harvard University Press.

Seagrave, D., & Grisso, T. (2002). Adolescent development and the measurement of juvenile psychopathy. *Law and Human Behavior*, *26*, 219–239.

Shaffer, J. N., & Ruback, R. B. (2002). Violent victimization as a risk factor for violent offending among juveniles. *Juvenile Justice Bulletin*.

Washington, DC: U.S. Department of Justice, Office of Justice Programs, Office of Juvenile Justice and Delinquency Prevention. Retrieved November 8, 2019, from https://www.ncjrs.gov/pdffiles1/ojjdp/195737.pdf.

Sharkey, P., Torrats-Espinosa, G., & Takyara, D. (2017). Community and the crime decline: The causal effect of local nonprofits on violent crime. *American Sociological Review, 82*, 1214–1240.

Sheidow, A., McCart, M., & Davis, M. (2016). Multisystemic therapy for emerging adults with serious mental illness and justice involvement. *Cognitive Behavioral Practice, 23*, 356–367.

Shin, R. Q., Smith, L. C., Welch, J. C., & Ezeorfor, I. (2016). Is Allison more likely than Lakisha to receive a callback from counseling professionals? A racism audit study. *The Counseling Psychologist, 44*, 1187–1211.

Shoemaker, D. (2010). *Theories of delinquency* (6th ed.). New York, NY: Oxford University Press.

Shufelt, J., & Cocozza, J. (2006). *Youth with mental health disorders in the juvenile justice system: Results from a multi-state, multi-system prevalence study.* Delmar, NY: National Center for Mental Health and Juvenile Justice.

Shulman, E. P., & Cauffman, E. (2013). Reward-biased risk appraisal and its relation to juvenile versus adult crime. *Law and Human Behavior, 37*, 412–423.

Skeem, J., Manchak, S., & Peterson, J. (2011). Correctional policy for offenders with mental illness: Creating a new paradigm for recidivism reduction. *Law and Human Behavior, 35*, 110–126.

Skeem, J., Monahan, J., & Mulvey, E. (2002). Psychopathy, treatment involvement, and subsequent violence among civil psychiatric patients. *Law and Human Behavior, 26*, 577–603.

Skinner, H. (1982). The Drug Abuse Screening Test. *Addiction Behavior, 7*, 363–371.

Smith, A., Steinberg, L., Strang, N., & Chein, J. (2015). Age differences in the impact of peers on adolescents' and adults' neural response to reward. *Developmental Cognitive Neuroscience, 11*, 75–82.

Sorensen, J., & Cunningham., M. (2010). Conviction offense and prison violence: A comparative study of murderers and other offenders. *Crime & Delinquency, 56*, 103–125.

Sparrow, S., Cicchetti, D., & Balla, D. (2005). *Vineland-II Adaptive Behavior Scales.* Circle Pines, MN: AGS Publishing.

Spector, R. (2001). Is there racial bias in clinicians' perceptions of the dangerousness of psychiatric patients? A review of the literature. *Journal of Mental Health, 10*(1), 5–15.

Steinberg, A., Brymer, M., Decker, K., & Pynoos, R. (2004). The UCLA PTSD reaction index. *Current Psychiatry Reports, 6*, 96–100.

Steinberg, L. (2008). A social neuroscience perspective on adolescent risk-taking. *Developmental Review, 28*, 78–106.

Steinberg, L. (2009). Should the science of adolescent brain development inform public policy? *American Psychologist*, *64*, 739–750.

Steinberg, L. (2010). A dual systems model of adolescent risk-taking. *Developmental Psychobiology*, *52*, 216–224.

Steinberg, L. (2013). The influence of neuroscience on U.S. Supreme Court decisions involving adolescents' criminal culpability. *Nature Reviews Neuroscience*, *14*, 513–518.

Steinberg, L. (2014). *The age of opportunity: Lessons from the new science of adolescence*. New York, NY: Houghton Mifflin Harcourt.

Steinberg, L. (2017). *Adolescence* (11th ed.). New York: McGraw Hill.

Steinberg, L., & Cauffman, E. (1996). Maturity of judgment in adolescence: Psychosocial factors in adolescent decision making. *Law and Human Behavior*, *20*, 249–272.

Steinberg, L., Cauffman, E., Woolard, J., Graham, S., & Banich, M. (2009). Are adolescents less mature than adults? Minors' access to abortion, the juvenile death penalty, and the alleged APA "flip-flop." *American Psychologist*, *64*, 583–594.

Steinberg, L., Graham, S., O'Brien, L., Woolard, J., Cauffmann, E., & Banich, M. (2009). Age differences in future orientation and delay discounting. *Child Development*, *80*, 26–44.

Steinberg, L., & Monahan, K. C. (2007). Age differences in resistance to peer influence. *Developmental Psychology*, *43*, 1531–1543.

Steinberg, L., & Scott, E. (2003). Less guilty by reason of adolescence: Developmental immaturity, diminished responsibility, and the juvenile death penalty. *American Psychologist*, *58*, 1009–1018.

Strand, V., Sarmiento, T., & Pasquale, L. (2005). Assessment and screening tools for trauma in children and adolescents: A review. *Trauma, Violence and Abuse*, *6*, 55–78.

Strathman, A., Gleicher, F., Boninger, D., & Edwards, C. (1994). The consideration of future consequences: Weighing immediate and distant outcomes of behavior. *Journal of Personality and Social Psychology*, *66*, 742–752.

Tanenhaus, D. (2004). *Juvenile justice in the making*. New York, NY: Oxford University Press.

Taylor, C. S., & Smith, P. R. (2013). The attraction of gangs: How can we reduce it? In T. R. Simon, N. M. Ritter, & R. R. Mahendra (Eds.), *Changing course: Preventing gang membership* (pp. 19–30). Washington, DC: National Institute of Justice.

Teplin, L., Abram, K., McClelland, G., Dulcan, M., & Mericle, A. (2002). Psychiatric disorders in youth in juvenile detention. *Archives of General Psychiatry*, *59*, 1133–1143.

Tillbrook, C., Mumley, D., & Grisso, T. (2003). Avoiding expert opinions on the ultimate legal question: The case for integrity. *Journal of Forensic Psychology Practice*, *3*(3), 77–87. doi:10.1300/J158v03n03_05

Tolan, P. (2007). Understanding violence. In D. Flannery, A. Versonyi, & J. Waldman (Eds.), *The Cambridge handbook of violent behavior and aggression* (pp. 5–18). Cambridge, UK: Cambridge University Press.

Toupin, J. (1993). Adolescent murderers: Validation of a typology and study of their recidivism. In A. Wilson (Ed.), *Homicide: The victim/offender connection* (pp. 135–156). Cincinnati, OH: Anderson Publishing Co.

Tremblay, R., Nagin, D, Sequin, J., Zoccolillo, M., Zelazo, P., Borvin, M., Perusse, D., & Japel, C. (2004). Physical aggression during early childhood: Trajectories and predictors. *Pediatrics, 114*, 43–50.

Trulson, C., Caudill, J., Haerle, D., & DeLisi, M. (2012). Cliqued up: The postincarceration recidivism of young gang-related homicide offenders. *Criminal Justice Review, 37*, 174–190.

Valencia, R., & Suzuki, L. (2000). *Intelligence testing and minority students: Foundations, performance factors, and assessment issues.* New York: Sage.

Vieira, T., Skilling, T., & Peterson-Badali, M. (2009). Matching court-ordered services with treatment needs: Predicting treatment success with young offenders. *Criminal Justice and Behavior, 36*, 385–401.

Viljoen, J., Brodersen, E., Shaffer, C., & McMahon, R. (2016). Risk reduction interventions for adolescent offenders. In K. Heilbrun, D. DeMatteo, & N. E. S. Goldstein (Eds.), *APA handbook of psychology and juvenile justice* (pp. 517–544). Washington, DC: American Psychological Association.

Vincent, G., & Hart, S. (2012). Legal uses and assessment of psychopathy. In D. Faust (Ed.), *Coping with psychiatric and psychological testimony* (6th ed., pp. 563–586). New York, NY: Oxford University Press.

Vincent, G., Kimonis, E., & Clark, A., (2016). Juvenile psychopathy: Appropriate and inappropriate uses in legal proceedings. In K. Heilbrun, D. DeMatteo, & N. E. S. Goldstein (Eds.), *APA handbook of psychology and juvenile justice* (pp. 197–232). Washington, DC: American Psychological Association.

Vries, A., & Liem, M. (2011). Recidivism of juvenile homicide offenders. *Behavioral Science & the Law, 29*, 483–498.

Wasserman, G., Reynolds, L., Lucas, C., Fisher, P., & Santos, L. (2002). The Voice DISC-IV with incarcerated male youths: Prevalence of disorder. *Journal of the American Academy of Child and Adolescent Psychiatry, 41*, 314–321.

Weathers, F. W., Blake, D. D., Schnurr, P. P., Kaloupek, D. G., Marx, B. P., & Keane, T. M. (2013). *The Clinician-Administered PTSD Scale for DSM-5 (CAPS-5)*. [Assessment] Available from www.ptsd.va.gov.

Weisburd, D., Farrington, D. P., Gill, C., Ajzenstadt, M., Bennett, T., Bowers, K., Caudy, M. S., Holloway, K., Johnson, S., Losel, F., Mallender, J., Perry, A., Tang, L. L., Taxman, F., Telep, C., Tierney, R., Tto, M. M., Watson, C., Wilson, D. B., & Wooditch, A. (2017).

What works in crime prevention and rehabilitation: An assessment of systematic reviews. *Criminology & Public Policy, 16*(2), 415–449.

Wevodau, A. (2016). *Review of trauma screening tools for children and adolescents.* National Youth Screening and Assessment Partners. http://www.nysap.us/Products.html.

Wilson, D., Bouffard, L., & Mackenzie, D. (2005). A quantitative review of structured, group-oriented, cognitive-behavioral programs for offenders. *Criminal Justice and Behavior, 32*, 172–204.

Wolfgang, M., Figlio, R., & Sellin, T. (1972). *Delinquency in a birth cohort.* Chicago, IL: University of Chicago Press.

Woolard, J., & Fountain, E. (2016). Serious questions about serious juvenile offenders' patterns of offending and offenses. In K. Heilbrun, D. DeMatteo, & N. E. S. Goldstein (Eds.), *APA handbook of psychology and juvenile justice* (pp. 141–157). Washington, DC: American Psychological Association.

Yudko, E., Lozhkina, O., & Fouts, A. (2007). A comprehensive review of the psychometric properties of the Drug Abuse Screening Test. *Journal of Substance Abuse Treatment, 32*, 189–198.

Zapf, P. A., Kukucka, J., Kassin, S. M., & Dror, I. E. (2018). Cognitive bias in forensic mental health assessment: Evaluator beliefs about its nature and scope. *Psychology, Public Policy, and Law, 24*(1), 1–10. doi:10.1037/law0000153

Zappala, M., Reed, A. L., Beltrani, A., Zapf, P. A., & Otto, R. K. (2018). Anything you can do, I can do better: Bias awareness in forensic evaluators. *Journal of Forensic Psychology Research & Practice, 18*(1), 45–56.

Zara, G., & Farrington, D. (2013). Assessment of risk of juvenile compares with adult criminal onset: Implications for policy, prevention, and intervention. *Psychology, Public Policy and Law, 19*, 235–249.

Zelechoski, A. (2016). Trauma, adverse experience, and offending. In K. Heilbrun, D. DeMatteo, & N. E. S. Goldstein (Eds.), *APA handbook of psychology and juvenile justice* (pp. 325–342). Washington, DC: American Psychological Association.

Zuckerman, M., Eysenck, S., & Eysenck, H. (1978). Sensation seeking in England and America: Cross-cultural, age, and sex comparisons. *Journal of Consulting and Clinical Psychology, 46*, 139–149.

Zwartz, M. (2018). Report writing in the forensic context: Recurring problems and the use of a checklist to address them. *Psychiatry, Psychology and Law, 25*(4), 578–588.

Index

Tables are indicated by an italic *t* following the page/paragraph number.

For the benefit of digital users, indexed terms that span two pages (e.g., 52–53) may, on occasion, appear on only one of those pages.